ENDORSEMENTS

Joan Donaldson's prose sings. It is wonderfully alive
with the details and rituals of her life and work on her
husband's family farm. It sings with the beauty and
rewards of the land she has committed to. Above all it
sings with an uncommon integrity, never slipping into easy
sentimentality, never slighting the hard work and even
drudgery such a life demands, yet finding fulfillment and
dignity in even the most common tasks - so that we come
away from this book filled not just with admiration, but
with a bit of envy as well.

Perhaps the book's most remarkable achievement is to
convince us that a life of simplicity and commitment to
land and community can engage and nourish an intelligent,
curious, analytical, and creative mind. Donaldson is
joyfully wedded to the land, in all its joys and trials, and
this is her epithalamion.

Robert Finch, Co-editor of The Norton Book of Nature
Writing in the English Tradition, and author of The Death
of a Hornet, The Iambics of Newfoundland and A Cape
Cod Notebook

Whether she's writing about the staccato of a hairy woodpecker echoing through the woods, tapping sweet sap from a cluster of maples during a spring sugaring ritual or mourning the loss of her ox, Tolstoy, Joan Donaldson's sensuous prose shimmers and surprises. Donaldson's collection of essays, *Wedded to the Land* peels back the skin of her blueberry farm with the precision and eloquence of a Wendell Berry, Edward Abbey and other agrarian essayists who make us pine for the lost heart of the country.
George Getschow, Writer-in-Residence & Conference Director, The Mayborn Graduate Institute of Journalism and former editor for The Wall Street Journal

In the hands of Joan Donaldson, a family farm comes beautifully and sometimes painfully to life. Her pages are filled with ripening peaches, with blueberry bushes whipped by an unforgiving wind, a farmer grieving over the loss of a beloved ox. Donaldson never gives way to easy sentiment; she invites her readers to experience the hard-won joys and inevitable sorrows of a life lived in synch with nature.
Cathleen Medwick
Literary Editor, MORE Magazine, and author of *Teresa of Avila*

Joan Donaldson is a pure, profound, and meaningful writer often expounding on topics that are close to her own heart; therefore, her words are carefully considered and thoughtfully brought to life.
Jill Peterson, Editor of *A Simple Life* Magazine, author of *Homestead, Homecoming* and *The Settlement*

WEDDED TO THE LAND

ADDITIONAL BOOKS
BY JOAN DONALDSON

The Real Pretend, illustrated by Tasha Tudor

A Pebble and A Pen

The Secret of the Red Shoes, illustrated by Doris Ettlinger

On Viney's Mountain

Her essays can be found in these anthologies:

At Home in the Garden

Home for Christmas

Ten Spurs, volumes 1 and 2

WEDDED TO THE LAND

Stories From a Simple Life on an Organic Fruit Farm

JOAN DONALDSON

WESTBOW
P R E S S
A DIVISION OF THOMAS NELSON

WestBow Press books may be ordered through booksellers or by contacting:

WestBow Press
A Division of Thomas Nelson
1663 Liberty Drive
Bloomington, IN 47403
www.westbowpress.com
1-(866) 928-1240

Because of the dynamic nature of the Internet, any web addresses or links contained in
this book may have changed since publication and may no longer be valid. The views
expressed in this work are solely those of the author and do not necessarily reflect the
views of the publisher, and the publisher hereby disclaims any responsibility for them.

Any people depicted in stock imagery provided by Thinkstock are models,
and such images are being used for illustrative purposes only.

Certain stock imagery © Thinkstock.

ISBN: 978-1-4497-8550-5 (sc)
ISBN: 978-1-4497-8549-9 (e)
ISBN: 978-1-4497-8551-2 (hc)

Library of Congress Control Number: 2013902891

Printed in the United States of America

WestBow Press rev. date: 4/8/2013

TABLE OF CONTENTS

For my grandparents Peter and Marie Schnoor
and their three daughters,
Ruth, Elfreida, Gretchen.

"Speak to the earth and it shall teach thee,"
Job 12:8

ACKNOWLEDGMENTS

I owe immense gratitude and blessings to my family and friends who encouraged me to collect and publish my creative nonfiction. A special thank you to John, Kay and Lisa who edited this work, and to my mother, Ruth who provided me with copies of my published works. I'm not that organized. And to Anne, forever my first reader.

Thank you to Sena Jeter Naslund, Kathleen Driscoll, Karen Mann, and Katy Yocum for creating the Spalding University MFA program that nurtured my talents. And thank you to my mentors, Bob Finch, Roy Hoffman, and Cathy Medwick for your wonderful advice and to my fellow alumni.

Thank you to George Getschow, Dr. Mitch Land, Joann Ballentine, and Sarah Wyman for establishing the Mayborn Literary Nonfiction Conference that continues to cultivate my writing skills. Thank you to the Mayborn Graduate Institute of Journalism for permission to publish the essays, *Teamwork* and *Saint George and the Dragon* that first appeared in *Ten Spurs*, and for giving me that joyous moment when *Saint George* won the Hearst 2007 Nonfiction Prize for Literary Excellence. I am honored to be part of this literary tribe.

Thank you to the good editors, Owen Thomas and Judy Lowe of *The Christian Science Monitor*. Most of the shorter essays first appeared in *The Home Forum* and many of the longer pieces grew out of other essays that the *Monitor* published. Your affirmation gave me the confidence to endure the rejection slips.

Thank you to Jill Peterson for adopting me into *The Simple Life* family.

Thank you to Deborah and Louie Schakel for taking and supplying countless photographs. Without you, our albums would be empty. A special thank you to Louie for taking the cover photos.

Thank you to *Rosebud* magazine for publishing *Dignity*

Thank you to Carlos, who provides grist for storytelling.

Thank you to the staff at the Maranatha Christian Writers Conference for choosing my manuscript as the winner of your book contest.

And above all, thanks be to God, to Him be the glory.

PORTALS

The afternoon John introduced me to his parent's farm, fog rose off the dwindling drifts of snow. Our boots slipped in the crystalline slush, gray with dirt churned up by tractor tires. We slogged past tattered stalks of asparagus ferns; sculpted by snow into tawny shuttlecocks, and skirted the cherry orchards as John guided me down to the blueberry bog. Low cirrus clouds like wet fleece blanketed the sky. Silence sifted around us, sharpening my hearing, attuned to the sounds of our college campus.

I had dreamt of becoming a farmer, but my vision was smaller than the four hundred acres spread out before us. I wanted a log cabin, a cow, a garden with a few fruit trees, and of course, chickens scratching between rows of sweet corn. Sitting in geology classes, John had told me about his family's farm, but I had concentrated on his broad shoulders and the cracked skin on his hands. Now, we trudged the farm lane that bordered the woods, and cut through the hillside to reveal a thin layer of humus. Tree roots crusted with lichens snarled out of the underlying sand, and moss furred the exposed dirt. Chick-a-dees flitted through Scotch pines. At the base of the hill, we walked out into a flat basin about a quarter of a mile wide and filled with row after row of blueberry bushes that stretched for almost a mile.

"These are the blueberries." John swept his arm in an arc, as if he introduced me to a host of cousins and uncles. "They thrive in this peat bog. In some places, the peat is thirty feet thick."

Like many peat bogs, perhaps this one began as a depression filled with water from a melting chunk of ice shed by the glaciers that deposited moraines rimming the fen. Waves had rippled over the shallow basin where Ojibwa and Ottawa once camped, leaving behind broken arrowheads and hatchets. Sedges and reeds fringed the shore along with shrubby pussy willows. Wild roses hedged the banks, and their pink blossoms starred the thickets laced with thorns. Over the decades, matted and decomposing grasses sank and the lake narrowed. The feet of wood ducks and red winged blackbirds carried in the seeds of other aquatic plants and even bits of mosses. Furry tangles of sphagnum mosses expanded over the pond's surface and flourished in the sunlight, creating floating masses of vegetation. As the upper layer of sphagnum grew, the bottom strata died, settling upon the lake's bottom. Trapped by water, hidden from sunshine, the vegetation decomposed more slowly and turned into peat, while other feathery mosses crept along the shore.

Slowly, swamp maple and wild cherries took root in the

mucky soil, their roots spread latterly across and through the mat of mosses. When toppled by gale winds, they lifted disks of peat twelve feet in diameter. As a child, John rode his pony near the edge of the pond that continued to fill with sphagnum moss, rotting maple leaves and twigs. Snapping turtles skittered away from the pony's hooves and splashed into the liquid tinted amber from the groundwater flowing through the peat.

The ancient Celts and other northern Europeans believed that bogs were portals to another world, to a land of gods and goddesses. Sometimes they flung silver goblets or swords into bogs to mollify their god, and during famines the Celts even sacrificed their royalty to appease the fertility goddess. They mutilated their lord's body and slipped him into the floating mass of sphagnum moss that can hold water up to twenty-times its own weight.

"My grandfather bought this farm in 1937, at the end of the Depression," John said. "He saw that his neighbors to the east had several acres in blueberries, so granddad and my uncles planted a couple of acres."

John's grandfather shifted the gears of his tractor and his plow shoved aside mounds of crumbling brown peat. A hidden community of micro bacteria, insect larvae, and mycelium flourished in the mounds, and a curious smell rose from the ancient organic matter, an odd mixture of bay laurel, cloves and timothy. Voles skittered through grassy tunnels away from the tractor's tires. Deer watched from the sassafras thickets skirting the bog.

Dressed in pleated beige pants and white tee-shirt, one son's hands dropped the rooted blueberry cuttings into the shallow trench every five feet. With his boots, another son scraped soil around their roots and heeled the plants into the peat that smelled like cloves. The high bush blueberry cuttings grew eight or ten foot high. Numerous shoots spread around the base of the bush; as the canes thickened, they created gray crowns rising from the peat. For the next few years, John's grandfather and uncles weeded between the bushes, pruned them in the winter and mixed up sprays to keep away pests. Instead of goblets and nobility, they sacrificed fifteen-hours a day to bring forth their first harvest.

Finally, the summer arrived when father and sons oversaw the dozens of migrants who drove north from Missouri and Arkansas. Their southern voices hovered between the rows as their fingers reached into bushes and rustled leaves. Blueberries plunked into metal lard buckets tied to their waists with baling twine. At noon, the pickers chugged quarts of buttermilk and bit into chunks of cornbread.

Red bandanas wreathed John's college-aged mother and aunts' heads as they stood in the shade, clad in dungarees and plaid blouses. Their tan fingers lifted buckets and poured a stream of blue into pint berry boxes. They teased and laughed about their beaus while fitting twelve pints into wooden rectangular boxes called flats. When evening shadowed the bog, cool air sank and curled between the flats, chilling the berries. The next morning, the brothers stacked them on trucks with round noses that hauled their bounty to Grand Junction, Michigan, and from that small village, the blueberries traveled to Chicago and beyond.

One by one, the siblings dropped away, like dry beans falling from a brittle pod. They ventured into new careers, new towns, new states. One fall afternoon their gray-haired parents slipped into their sedan, and motored north towards Holland to visit their married daughter Mary and her two sons. At a Y in the road, John's grandfather didn't notice the car rounding the curve. Glass and steel smashed. Bodies hurled. Hearts exploded. Hands stiffened.

After the last shovel full of dirt rounded the mounds over the parents' graves, after churchwomen's hands brushed away the cake crumbs, and washed coffee cups, the siblings drove back to their careers. But John's mother, Mary packed her family's belongings and returned to the land.

Now, John and I walked beside thousands of blueberry bushes that he and his parents had added to his grandparent's farm. Staring at the bushes, I wondered why John had brought me to this bog. I didn't like blueberries. I still don't. But thirty-seven years later, I understand why.

FLUENCY

"For behold, the winter is past...
The time has arrived for pruning."
Song of Solomon 2: 11-12

John and I married in October and moved into a one bedroom apartment, half of a duplex that had been built to house migrants. Fake brown paneling smothered the walls; beige linoleum covered a cold cement floor. I had crawled into a walnut shell still rank with the bitter smell of its green husk. Back at college I had left a trail of yellow rooms, so I painted the window trim and the cabinet doors yellow. My braided rug and quilts splattered colors that lifted the gloom while traditional fiddle music stirred the air.

That winter, the winds off of Lake Michigan whipped snow into wraiths that swirled across the open fields; the drifts rose to our windowsills and buried our Datsun. Scenes from *The Long Winter* flitted through my mind when I stared into the whiteness, and no longer did *The Little House* books seem romantic. Rural winters are snow leopards that pounce upon the landscape. They shake their prey, scattering isolation and loneliness. John's childhood friends had fled and none returned after college. So we read tidbits to each other from Louis Bromfield's writings about organic farming and gathered ideas to implement on our land. While eating bowls of potato soup and slabs of fresh bread, we discussed Wendell Berry's articles in *The New Farm* and shaped a vision of a nurturing healthy soils, sturdy blueberry bushes, and trading labor with future friends…whom we later discovered settling homesteads along the gravel roads of Allegan County.

Like any gardener yearning for spring, I sank into the seed catalogs, memorizing our farm's zone and normal amount of growing days. My tomato vocabulary expanded to include words such as indeterminate and determinate. But I shook my head one morning in late April when John tossed out terms that I had never heard.

"The peach trees are at balloon pink," John said.

"What's that?" I lifted my plate and licked the film of maple syrup and butter that marbleized the china.

"Balloon pink describes how swollen the buds are and tells the stage of development; they're almost ready to bloom. It's a farming term, like king bloom or shuck split."

"Shuck split? Who thinks up these words?" The term conjured an image of a milkweed pod foaming fluff. I rolled the words around in my mouth, feeling my tongue on the back of my teeth.

"Shuck split is when the dry husk falls off the blossom and exposes the tiny, green peach."

Every discipline has its particular vocabulary. Although I had studied German, Spanish and Russian, agriculture demanded a fluency in techniques and descriptions absent from my urban and academic experiences. John's vocabulary flowed from his awareness of how blueberries grew or the way a piece of equipment functioned.

After breakfast, we trudged past the two story gray-shingled shop full of a spectrum of tools necessary to maintain a farm. In one day, John might need to weld a coupling, or replace the teeth on the tractor size rototiller.

"How do you know how to do everything?" I asked. "Weld, fix a conveyor belt? Build a pole building." At times, cultural shock blew over me, like the snowdrifts that had smothered the asparagus fields.

"Our hired hand taught me. Farmers have to be a Jack-of-all-trades," he replied.

My father's hands had guided mine, teaching me to miter wood, hit nails, and create furniture for my dollhouse. My mother had showed me how to weed in her vegetable garden, but my enthusiasm had disappeared when I discovered that spiders lurked beneath the leaves.

"Hop on," John said. I sat on the fender of a tractor, and we rumbled past peach and cherry orchards and down to the blueberry bog. He parked the tractor at the beginning of a row.

"Good place for you to learn to drive a tractor. We'll be moving it along the row, using it to power the hydraulic pruners."

I slid onto the seat, eying the various gauges and levers.

"Push in the clutch, make sure both the high and low gears are in neutral, and turn the key," John said.

I followed his instructions. Nothing happened.

"You're too short. Clutch's not far enough in."

I slumped in the seat, shoved all my weight on the clutch, shifted the gears into neutral, and the Massey Ferguson's engine turned over. Across the dash jiggled gauges labeled by little drawings instead of words. A secret agrarian code, perhaps?

"Can't farmers read?" I asked. A rabbit and a tortoise clued the driver as to how to increase or decrease the speed.

"The builders use universal symbols because they ship tractors overseas. That's the throttle lever; leave it where it is, for now."

"What's that?"

"PTO lever."

"What does that mean?"

"Power Take Off, a shaft that powers equipment such as mowers, spray rigs, balers. Pretty dangerous. We should have the shield cover on it so that it won't catch on my pants and tear off my leg."

When my family had driven along back roads admiring orchards and hay fields, agriculture had never appeared dangerous, but since marrying John, I had noticed caution symbols slapped onto equipment. *Achtung* blazed in red letters beneath the figure of a man falling off the forklift, warning people not to ride on the front tines. Or a hand slashed by a line alerted farmers not to stick their fingers into a bailer. To avoid these practices seemed obvious to me, but farmers are risk takers who annually gamble against nature and sometimes ignore potential dangers. Too often, John tramped through the door with small rips on his pants or slices in his work boots.

"Chain saw got me," he would say and laugh it off.

I patched his pants with denim and prayers, trusting that his guardian angels would continue to shield him the next time he flipped over a bulldozer while grading a ditch bank. His parents told stories of a friend killed when he fell, and his tractor rolled over him. Such tales brewed my respect for equipment.

John fiddled with the gears. "Try again; pull ahead about three bushes."

Sitting cockeyed, pressing all my weight on the clutch, I turned the key. The engine grumbled, and the tractor crept along the grassy strip. After three bushes, I pressed the brake, but the tractor rolled onward. Not enough weight.

"Stop!" John called. "Too far!"

I jammed down the clutch, shifted into neutral, and turned the key off. The tractor still purred. "How do you turn it off?"

"Pull the knob on the left." John jogged up and tugged.

"How come they didn't label it? Why didn't they paint a sign with a slashed tractor? Or is this common knowledge?"

"I think the drawing got rubbed off. Get off. I'll back this up so we can run the hydraulics."

"Tractors are a nuisance. Noisy. Smelly. Couldn't we use old fashion, people powered pruners?"

John backed the tractor up and parked it. He removed two loppers with wooden handles hanging on a bar behind the tractor seat.

"OK, we'll do it the old fashioned way. More keeping with organic ideas. But eventually you'll get the hang of driving a tractor."

"I'd rather learn to drive draft animals. A team of horses or oxen." I stared at a blueberry bush bristling with suckers. "How do we do this?"

"First, you'll cut out most of the suckers. I'll follow and prune the thicker gray canes"

I circled the bush, snipping, pulling out the reedy suckers. Pruning is like creating a sculpture; after all, within the term agriculture abides the word culture. Before an artist raises his chisel, he envisions his creation, just as we pictured in our minds a bush with only a dozen sturdy canes so that sunlight could penetrate the leaves. I cut away most of the suckers, making the bush narrower and leaving those suckers that would eventually replace the older canes. Like most of farming activities, after pruning a couple of bushes or trees, the job either becomes drudgery or a pathway to rumination. While my muscles squeezed the loppers and threw branches into the path, I pondered Wendell Berry's argument that good farming requires spiritual discipline and a deepening relationship with the land. In the past, farming was called husbandry, a fitting expression because farmers are wedded to the soil. At the end of a row, we gazed back, and witnessed the difference created by our blades.

"What happens to the brush?"

"I'll bush hog it."

"What's does that mean?"

"A bush hog is a heavy duty mower that can chop up branches and throw the pieces several yards. Could wallop you in the head if you're standing too close."

"Lovely. Isn't there a less dangerous way?"

"Not really, plus the chopped up branches rot and return their nutrients back to the land."

One day I would catch on. I hung my pruners on the back of the tractor.

"Time for lunch. You take the tractor. I'll walk."

I headed home via a path through the woods. A few violet leaves poked through the leaf litter. On the top of the ridge, I looked down into the bog. In organic farming, everything rotted down to the farmer and his land.

My Immoderate Melon Man

After a week in our home, most seed catalogs flip open to the cantaloupe section, because John loves melons. I was alerted to his passion the first time we visited my parents. A slice of muskmelon smiled up from his plate, and he stared at it in disbelief. Later on the ride home he explained why.

"In my family we each eat a whole muskmelon or half of a watermelon." Despite John's motto, "everything in moderation" he claimed no moderation when consuming melons.

During one long, snowy, winter of perusing seed catalogs, John's melon "wish list" grew. I've always suspected that the photos displayed in the catalogs were taken with an orange filter in order to titillate a gardener's senses. John salivated when gazing at faithful varieties such as Ambrosia or Hales Jumbo, but other varieties also tempted his taste buds. Finally, I suggested that he till more ground for a special melon patch, and plant whatever he wished to sample, so that in the following years we could concentrate on two or three favorite varieties.

One April afternoon, I opened a dozen packets of cantaloupe seeds and a couple of watermelon and planted more than three flats of melons. Most of them germinated, but in vacant spots I popped in a seedling from another spot where two seeds had sprouted. Because spring time was a carnival with numerous demands, I tended to fuss with seedlings while swallowing a mug of tea before heading back to the fields. I didn't label the mismatched melons so along the way, the varieties mingled.

A melon was a melon to me, but not to the king of cantaloupes. When the globes yellowed and their scent filled the air, we scrambled to match the photos and descriptions with the ripe fruit. John was determined to decipher the mystery, but when the harvest averaged more than a dozen melons a day, it no longer mattered. Each meal began with muskmelon, and watermelons became the afternoon snack. John did not turn orange, but his spoon moved less hastily. True to my up-breeding, I ate my one slice.

Anyone who ventured on the farm went home with a cantaloupe, including the UPS driver. We hauled baskets of Crenshaws to the food coop meeting, and left fragrant French hybrids at friends' doors. When the flow dwindled, we stored a watermelon in the root cellar, and consumed it on a warm October day.

Yet by February, John stood in the grocery store staring at the mounded display of cantaloupes. He sniffed one, then another, as he analyzed the faint yellow appearing beneath the ribbing.

"Look," he said. "Two for the price of one. Can't beat that." He hefted two melons and placed them in my cart. The king of cantaloupes still reigned.

DIGNITY

"You shall not wrong a stranger or oppress him,
for you were strangers in the land of Egypt."
Exodus 22:21

On an August morning, the blueberry bog trapped the sun's heat.
The hot air and dust spun a haze that cloaked the narrow basin,
now edged by a row of migrants' cars. Rust had gnawed at the
bottom of the cars' doors, around headlights, and bumpers, and
several sported a white hood or gold door that contrasted with
the original color of the vehicle. I questioned our dependence
upon migrant labor to harvest fresh berries, and chided myself
for falling into the mire of perpetuating other people's poverty.
Yet my husband's family had always used transient labor, and due
to the recession of the late 1970's, many of our pickers could not
find other forms of work.

A score of children, both white-skinned and brown, from
toddlers to teens, wrestled in the backseats of cars, fiddled
with radios, or played in the sandy ruts of the farm road. The
preschoolers hovered over puddles, like a cloud of Swallowtail

butterflies. Mud streaked yellow and orange t-shirts or stained the seats of their blue and green shorts. A few girls tugged at drooping socks, and all wore dingy sneakers. Their parents had segregated into small groups and sat in the shade of a silver maple, waiting for the dew to dry off the blueberry bushes so that they could begin work. From a radio, a country music singer praised his pick-up; his voice wove between the southern accents and Spanish words. Some of the pickers were immigrants from Missouri and Arkansas who had settled in Michigan, while others had driven north from Mexico or Texas for the summer. In a few minutes, they would scatter between the rows, their chatter blending with the prattle of the brown thrasher and the buzz of the cicadas.

As a college-educated, newly married twenty-four-year-old, I found packing blueberries a boring job. I stood in the shade of a tin roof, folding and fitting together cardboard boxes that would hold twelve pints of blueberries. A hired hand who worked for my in-laws had built the portable packing shed from corrugated tin onto a rectangular four-wheel trailer. The shed's longest sides could be lifted to form two awnings that protected me from the sun. Earlier this morning, John had stacked large containers of cellulose pints, picking buckets, yellow plastic packing flats, and bundles of cardboard flats onto the flatbed. When we needed to move and pick another field, we loaded up the tables, and the ancient Massey Ferguson tractor hauled the swaying contraption through the bog. Like some gypsy caravan, we would set up camp at a new location and pull off our equipment.

My fingers had memorized how to fit the cardboard tabs into their slits, fold over the flaps and construct a shallow flat. Once you've made one flat, what else is there to learn about the process? So I watched the crowd. Emma, her husband, Bud, and three-year-old daughter had rattled north from Florida in their blue Fairlane and unpacked their bundles in a migrant cabin. Dressed in jeans with a gray t-shirt bulging over his beer belly, Bud sat on a bucket, coughing. Nine months pregnant, with a scraggly pony tail, Emma wore stretch pants and maternity top bleached so often that its flowers were gray. She leaned against a trailer tire, and watched her daughter as she pushed a toy car across the dirt. Soon Emma's long fingers would rake berries into buckets that Bud would carry to the receiving table.

"Hope I can pick my hundred pounds," she drawled. "Baby due any day. Have to lay off for a week."

I admired Emma's tenacity. She reminded me of the women I had met while volunteering in Eastern Tennessee, a breed of women as gritty as cornbread and as sweet as sorghum. Yet I wondered why she never expressed a yearning for a permanent home, or a husband motivated to work a reliable job that would support their family. The boundaries of her life experiences restricted her dreams, and I knew that my expectations would be as foreign to her as the tabouli I ate for lunch. Emma might want a better future for her children, but she would shy away from my suggestions to learn skills for a higher paying job. So I had bought her a package of diapers and a yellow receiving blanket, a hint of color for the soon-to-arrive baby.

"I hope you do rest for a week." I plunked a dozen flats on the trailer.

"Guess I'll take me six buckets," Emma said. "'Less you'll let me pick into a lug." She glanced at me, violet eyes hopeful, one stained hand rested on her belly.

Pickers preferred pouring their full buckets into a rectangular plastic lug so that they would have to trudge less often to the receiving table. But for the person grading the fruit, dumping berries from a bucket onto a sorting screen required less strength than lifting a lug filled with thirty or forty pounds of fruit. If I allowed Emma to take a lug, the other pickers would squabble and demand the same concession. Some might even drive away, refusing to work. The number of pickers waiting to work would barely be sufficient to pick today's order, but I handed Emma a yellow lug.

"Why don't you walk down to the far end of the row. Keep out of sight, and start picking in about fifteen minutes. The bushes should be dry by then."

Emma nodded at Bud. He took their daughter's hand and followed as Emma waddled down the long row, her lug tucked under an arm. I heaved a bundle of flats onto the table and struggled to snap the thin plastic band binding the stack. A teenage boy strolled over and flashed a switchblade.

"Need help, ma'am?" Bobby Jackson jerked his thin wrist and the strap fell away. Gangly, in his white t-shirt and black jeans, he was a shadow of crisscrossed branches. In a city, Bobby would have joined a gang, but the confines of the country restricted him to slouching beneath the awning at the Tastee Freeze, smoking and eying the girls.

The Jackson brood lived in a house trailer near the township dump. Rust stains streaked the white siding; bikes sprawled in the dirt driveway littered with junked cars. Friends who lived a quarter of a mile away sometimes called the police when the Jackson's shouts and screams fractured the twilight call of whip-poor-wills. During August, their station wagon, held together with baling wire, bumped down Blueberry Hill. Five or six children spilled out, opened up a wheelchair and lifted from the backseat a brother in his twenties, and settled him into his chair. Throughout the day, they rolled the skinny man from one shady spot to another; his black hair flopped around his shoulders, his fingers clawed the armrests. Their father worked a factory job; picking berries provided cash for the family. Mrs. Jackson sat on a bucket near the wheelchair; her two tight pigtails curled away from her pudgy face, she drummed on the bottom of another bucket.

"Thank you." I watched Bobby click the knife close and slip it into his jean pocket. His cheeks needed no razor, and his hair, the color of oak bark, curled over the neck of his t-shirt. The outline of a cigarette pack bulged beneath a turned up sleeve. Was the knife a power symbol to impress his pals, or did he need a weapon in his rural realm of poverty? Even though I had attended a diverse city high school, I had strolled down its halls with other college bound friends, never encountering this restless class, but my husband had grown up playing with migrant children.

"I could help make them boxes, ma'am." Bobby's voice echoed his parents' Arkansas accent and softened his vowels. "Been watching." He snatched a flat and slapped it together. "Ain't hard."

"Thank you. I'd be glad for your help." I wanted to add, "I see you are a quick learner, you should finish high school, learn a trade". But I knew he wouldn't listen to this upstart from the city, and the lure of money would keep him in the fields. I knew one winter day I would spy him, unemployed, walking the back roads near Pullman.

"Hey, get your butts over here!" Bobby yelled at his siblings. "Come help the Boss Lady."

"Ma'am," Bobby's younger brother said. His jeans sported iron-on patches, their edges curled upward. "Mama says the bushes are dry. Can we start pickin'? Get goin' before it heats up any more?" Sleep had matted one side of his honey hair and dirt ringed his neck.

"Did you stick your arm into the center of the bush?" I asked. Wet berries would mold when packed into cellophane wrapped pints and shipped to Minneapolis. Pickers also needed to gently roll berries out of the clusters so the fruit would not become juicy. Nor should they drop leaves or small twigs into their buckets, skills I had developed in my first two years of marriage.

"Yes, ma'am. Berries are dry."

"Grab some buckets. Tell the others."

Tan arms shot out. Buckets swaying, T-shirts and jeans dashed away. Bobby tipped his head, grabbed the back of his brother's wheelchair and pushed him close to the row where his mother waited. She began picking.

Four young Mexican men selected a stack of buckets. In white button-down shirts, black trousers, and black leather shoes, they appeared dressed to wait tables in a restaurant instead of laboring in the sun. Yesterday they had rolled in to the field driving a maroon Buick. Their nervousness hinted that perhaps they had recently swum the Rio Grande, but in 1978, we asked no questions. Despite our rule that pickers received their week's earnings on Friday, this crew had approached John and me after their first day with outstretched hands.

"*Por favor*," one man had said. "*Dinero*." His black hair had glinted in the sunset, and he had stared at his cracked shoes, shoulders tense. An urgency pulsed from the men huddling together. They knew they begged.

John and I had glanced at each other. Should we break our rule and risk the ire of the other pickers? All of them would prefer a daily wage. One of the men had shifted his weight and looked up at us. His beagle's eyes severed my resolve. The men were strangers in a strange land where I still learned how to survive. My pride had never experienced such humbling, and I would probably never have to beg for money. I nodded at John.

"How much did they pick?" John had dug into his back pocket.

I had checked my record book. "A hundred pounds."

John had counted green bills into brown palms. The men's lungs expanded, faces softened. A stomach growled

"*Gracias, senor.*" The spokesman nodded his head. "*Muchas gracias.*"

The quartet had tumbled into a car and rumbled towards town. This morning I had discovered their car parked near the woods, where a gap in the sassafras trees created a slim harbor. A bag of sliced white bread rested in the rear window. Still dressed, the men slept. I had lowered my gaze and walked on. They were not the first squatters. Sometimes during the night, families snuck along the farm's roads and hid their station wagons in a secluded spot. Three or four children with matted hair slept in the back of the wagon while the parents snoozed on the front bench seat. After a night or two on this farm, they drifted away, avoiding the authorities who inspected labor camps and invaded fields searching for illegal immigrants.

Behind John's family home, a dozen of the migrants lived in a cluster of white clapboard cabins with tin roofs. Metal cots, a dinette set, gas stove, and kitchen sink filled the un-insulated houses. A cement block washhouse had replaced outhouses. During the summer, laundry rustled like sunflower leaves, pinned to lines that swooped between the cabins and leapt out to surrounding trees. Now and then on a Friday night, a squad car's headlights would blaze against a cabin's screened window, absorbing the rays of a single light bulb hanging from the ceiling. The officer would separate the brawl, confiscate knives, and tell the women to hide the booze. John had accepted the shadow of the migrant camp as a fact of farm life while my middle class upbringing questioned its existence.

Plink, plank, plunk, berries drummed the bottom of buckets. Leaves swished against shirtsleeves. Metal bails clinked against belt buckets. Voices darted between rows.

On top of Blueberry Hill, a band of children swarmed. Too young to pick, too small to tote buckets, they swirled like a cloud of gnats. A tangle of arms and legs, they rolled and tumbled through the grass. Their laughter mingled with the cricket's chirping. When tired, they collapsed in the shadow of the trailer; sweat beaded their upper lips and glistened on their necks. A chubby Hispanic girl fetched a Pepsi bottle filled with water, a communal jug passed hand to hand. Did they know that other children attended summer activities in parks or traveled with their families? As a child, I had weeded my mother's strawberries or picked beans, but I spent most of my summers in the shade, reading.

I pulled the last sleeve of pints from a container two feet high and four feet long that held about six hundred little boxes. My fingers tugged apart the green pints and fitted a dozen into a yellow plastic flat. At the receiving table, John lifted a bucket filled with twelve pounds of berries and dribbled a thin layer of fruit across a V-shaped screen built of hardware cloth. He shook the wooden sides of the screen, pulled out a soft berry, and poured the inspected fruit into a pint-filled flat. All afternoon we would repeat this process while pickers carried in buckets of berries. A few rows over, someone turned on a radio and pop music shook the quiet, while at the other end of the field a man yodeled a mariachi song. A cicada cleared its throat and interjected a drone.

"Hey, can we have that box?" a blonde-haired boy asked. Grass stains smeared the front of the t-shirt sticking to his ribcage.

"*Por favor, necesitamos,*" his comrade said, a black-eyed chipmunk peering over the table's edge.

A few of their parents packed a couple of toy trucks or cars, a doll or a handful of crayons. But for most pickers, the near empty gas tank, the baskets of laundry, and dwindling supply of pinto beans smothered concerns about education or toys. Although books and bikes eluded their children's hands, their imaginations bubbled.

"*Si, necesitan.*" I pushed the carton towards them. "Have fun."

"Let's go fishing!" the blonde-haired boy shouted.

The pudgy girl and another with a black ponytail, hopped into the box and cast imaginary lines. They reeled in catfish and bluegill. Giggles percolated. The cardboard tore at the upper edges. Feet pummeled the front panel. Legs thrashed

"I'm a bus driver," the ponytail girl said, and slipped into the driver's seat. The others scooted behind her and tucked their legs around each other. Gears growled. The box bounced as heads bobbed. The chubby girl waved; I waved back. They all grinned. Brakes squealed. The sides of the box buckled. The children flattened the container, hauled it to the top of the hill and sledded down. Childhood mined pleasure from our cast away container and the landscape.

Thirteen-year-old Lena marched up, thumped down a bucket, and plopped onto the trailer. She was a duckling bristling with pinfeathers, losing the down of childhood; Lena usually offered me more words than picked berries. Purple stains slicked the sides of her jeans where she had wiped her hands, and the back of her pink t-shirt had escaped her belt. Brown curly hair hid her face. Last Friday, she had darted about me like a dragonfly, saying that tomorrow she would spend the day with her father.

"How often do you see him?" I had asked.

"Once a year." She had swung a bucket back and forth.

"He lives far away?"

"Oh, no. He lives in Holland."

The jerk lived twenty minutes away and couldn't be bothered

to visit his daughter? My fingers had packed berries, but my heart had contracted. Didn't he realize that his daughter needed a father?

This morning, I noticed Lena's scowl and the slump of her shoulders.

"How'd the visit go with your dad?" I asked.

"He didn't come." Her words fell, flat as mowed grass. She rummaged in a brown bag stored under the trailer and pulled out a baloney sandwich. Picking up her bucket, Lena strode back to the bushes.

I wanted to shake the man by his collar. How dare he bruise her heart? Didn't he realize his rejection doomed her to seek affirmation elsewhere? With consistent kind words and guidance from her father, and Lena might finish high school and avoid an unwanted pregnancy. I slammed down a packed flat.

"Careful," John said. "Can't save them all."

But I wanted to, and vowed to listen even longer the next time Lena sat down to chat.

I fitted a cellophane wrapper over the top of a pint, slipped a rubber band over the crown of berries and placed the wrapped pint into one of the cardboard flats I had made. Swifter than the weaver's shuttle, my hands would repeat these motions all day. Dusky blueberries glistened beneath hundreds of cellophane wrappers, tucked into scores of flats. The tiers of white boxes printed with blue letters spelling *one dozen* expanded across the trailer like rising bread dough. By tomorrow, they would travel by refrigerated truck to Minneapolis.

Clutching three crayons, the chipmunk scampered up.

"*Por favor, papel?*" he asked.

"*Sí.*" From under the trailer, I pulled out a stack of saved cardboard and paper that had earlier encased the packages of cellophanes.

"*Gracias!*" He snatched the paper and skipped off to the shade where the other artists waited.

The sun arched overhead, and the air filled with the fragrance of blueberries. We brushed away deerflies and mosquitoes. Voices slid further down the rows, and red-faced pickers emerged carrying four or six buckets. Dark sweat stains streaked the backs of their shirts. About two o'clock, many of the crew slid into their cars and lumbered home. The songbirds slumbered. John and I sank onto the trailer bed, counting the number of flats that still needed to be filled for tomorrow's order.

"Should I go pick for awhile?" I stared at the heat waves shimmering along the road. The air was pudding, warm and gooey. "Not enough pickers left to bring in what we need."

"Nah, there's a lot of buckets out there. They don't want to walk up the long rows; they're waiting to bring them up when they quit. Wash your hands." John climbed into his pick up and drove off.

Why wash my hands? What was he planning? I worked the handle of the nearby pitcher pump and scrubbed off the juice. Dust billowed as John returned and parked his truck near the packing shed. He jumped out holding two familiar black cases and flipped open the lids.

John handed me my button box as he strapped on his red piano accordion. Its white keys shone against the glittering red plastic. He flicked a stop to open all the reeds, and the bellows hissed.

"What shall we play first? Reels or jigs?"

"Reels." I slipped a black leather strap over my right shoulder, my red box rested on my right knee, a ruby set with pearls. I ran my right hand fingers along the two rows of buttons, while my left thumb found the air valve. The bellows breathed.

We swung into *The Merry Blacksmith*. The young gnats flew from the shade and circled round us, staring. We raced into *The Congress* and ended with *Sally Gardens*.

"What is it?" The ponytail girl pointed at my red button box.

"An Irish accordion. It has buttons instead of piano keys." I squeezed the bellows and pushed out a C note. I drew them inward and a D flew out. "See, it plays a different note when I push and pull, like blowing into a harmonica."

"More. Play some more." The children ordered.

An older Mexican couple carrying four buckets materialized from between the rows. Gray peppered the man's black hair, followed by a plump woman in a flowered housedress.

"*Baile*?" He asked and raised his arms into ballroom position.

"Kerry polkas," John said. "Eagan's first."

We zipped into tunes composed in a mist-covered mountain corner of Ireland thousands of miles from Mexico. But the simple, clear voice of Kerry music spoke to the couples' feet. They reached for each other and whirled, trampling the grass, lifting the spicy scent from the peat. From the end of a row, Emma's husband slouched and smoked while she swung their toddler. Blonde and black-haired children snatched each other's hand and spun in a circle. More pickers trudged up to the shed and deposited their buckets. The wetback's stained hands clapped. Lena stared. John nodded at me, and we drew in our bellows.

"*Más!*" Everyone called. "More!"

John glanced at me. "How about *The Green Fields of America*?"

We rolled into the reel, and the air throbbed with a riot of notes written by another immigrant who had sailed from Ireland to America during a time when "No Irish Need Apply". Only the children skipped, as their parents sank onto the soil, closing their eyes. While their accents and languages emanated from different countries, these workers yearned for the same respect and hope that had drawn my ancestors from Scotland.

When the last notes rippled through the accordions' reeds, the sun had swung behind the woods. The worst of the afternoon heat had dissipated. The pickers cheered and swung empty buckets as they walked back into the bushes.

"*Gracias.*" The man smiled as he stooped for his bucket.

"*De nada.*" I smiled back, and slapped a cellophane onto another pint.

THE MUSIC OF
MILKING

"a good and spacious land,
a land flowing with milk and honey."
Exodus 3:8

John *thought* he was building a garage when he erected a timber-frame building only a stone's throw from the house we built in the middle of our farm. While washing the dishes, I mulled over how pleasant it would be to look out our kitchen window and watch goats lounge in a paddock. If goats lived in the new shed, the walk wouldn't be far when milking in the winter or during kidding season.

Once outside, I scanned the sixteen by twenty foot framework. "You know, a couple of goats would fit nicely in here. There's room for two stalls." John's hammer paused. I continued. "The aspens and honeysuckle on the north would shelter an outdoor pen." I tied on a nail apron.

John said nothing. Most likely he ruminated on how a few

years earlier I had wheedled him into a flock of chickens. My final bribe to make deviled eggs every day had nibbled away at his resolve. Not far from where we worked, our flock of Buff Orpingtons and Barred Rock hens scratched beneath a pin oak.

"We're not quite ready," John mumbled. "Some day." He moved the ladder over and gripped a board. His scarred leather boots thumped up the rungs. "Got it?" he asked as he positioned the top of the vertical board along the header.

I grabbed its edges. Using the toe of my work boot as a shim, I leveled the bottom of the board on the sill. In most situations, John was never ready to commit to a new responsibility while my feet waltzed away before the music even began. Yet eventually, he would pick up the rhythm and embrace my proposal.

While hammering, I reminded myself of the afternoon when John had hung up the phone and said. "We just bought a cow. Doug's neighbor bid on one for all of us. Let's go meet her."

A few minutes later, ten of us stood in a ring, staring at a Guernsey chewing her cud. No one had planned on a community cow. No one knew how to milk a cow. No one had a shed large enough to house a cow, but Doug offered a building site for a barn. We scrounged up materials, swatted nails, and within two weeks, Cindy Lou rested in clean straw. Despite admonitions from local farmers that no cow would tolerate being handled by ten pairs of hands, our community cow defied dairy logic. Yet one by one, the families in our cow co-op abandoned their homesteads and moved to cities for better paying jobs. Finally, John and I sold our share in the cow when Doug relocated to a southern state.

A few days later, I slipped home books from the library that explained the economic advantages of keeping goats. The evidence surrounded John that night when we huddled at our table, the glow of kerosene lamps falling upon the pages. The woodstove purred; the cats slept on the quilting frame.

"Did you know," I began, "that goats produce three times the amount of milk as a cow when you compare their milk production to the amount of food a cow eats?"

"But goat's milk doesn't separate naturally." John turned a page in his book.

"No, but it can be separated with a cream separator."

"But we don't own one, and they are expensive." John ran his fingers through his hair.

"Goats would be easier for me to handle." I studied the photo of an all white doe. "And think of the manure for the garden."

"Don't have a pasture."

"We could fence in the meadow east of the house," I suggested.

"I'm not ready. Too much other work."

Keeping a milk cow or goats is like stepping into a calculus problem. Because dairy animals must be milked at twelve hour intervals, three hundred days of the year, their needs would establish the boundaries of time and distance. When working at home, opening the barn door at the designated time is simple, but the length of a day trip from the farm is measured by the question: "Can we make it back in time to milk?" Dinner invitations from families without goats would necessitate an explanation of why we couldn't arrive until after we had completed chores. John and I understood these variables, but one spring evening a couple who kept goats invited us to share dinner. We strolled their farm, admiring the goat kids racing in the pasture as prettily as scene from *Heidi*.

"Such joie de vivre," I murmured.

"They are cute," John said.

A few weeks later, I heard John backing his pick-up next to the partially-built shed. A haystack of shiplap flooring shifted on the bed of the truck. We silently pulled the boards off and stacked them. Green sequin leaves dangled from the aspen trees, and plumes of lilacs drooped from a bush near the porch, their thick fragrance settled over us. A house wren trilled from the redbud tree where a few remaining mauve blossoms garlanded the branches, a perfect day to watch goats frolic.

"What's the flooring for," I asked, and noted a few two by fours jumbled at the bottom of the pile.

"A loft," John's straw hat hid his eyes. The board bounced as he dropped it on the stack.

"In a garage?"

"Have to store hay somewhere." John slammed the tailgate and pulled open the shed's doors. "How about we run the stalls for the goats on the west side?" He paced out the space. "And I thought the trees would make a good windbreak. I'll run their pen on the east side, along those lilacs."

"Great idea"

"And mark the page in that book with the plans for a goat stanchion. There should be enough of this flooring for the platform. I threw in a couple extra boards for the legs."

"Sure."

Our friends sold us a French Alpine doe, and Rosemary's full udder rocked as she trotted into the barn.

"Goats hate to be alone," I reminded John as he leaned over the stall and scratched Rosemary's head. "She needs a buddy."

The next day we drove home from another friend's barn with a white kid named Poppy. Out in their paddock, Poppy jumped off a granite rock and butted heads with Rosemary.

"Going to need hay," John said. "Guess I'll look for some used hay equipment."

"What do we need?"

"Haybine. Baler. Got a rake." He sighed. "Probably cheaper to buy milk."

Windrows of hay spiraled from the center of the five-acre field as if a giant cat had unwound a ball of bulky green yarn. The fragrance of alfalfa filled the thick evening air. Faint thunder growled over Lake Michigan five miles to the west while John and our friend Larry tinkered with the cantankerous baler. In June and July, the ancient International baler, its paint weathered to a rusty-red, had cheerfully spit out several hundred bales of first and second cutting hay. Now on August 1st, this cross-quarter day when the seasons danced away from the solstice and towards the fall equinox, our third cutting lay exposed, waiting for the men to unsnarl the baler's needle.

The humidity smothered us, pasting the hay chaff to our necks; I sat down on one of the bales the machine had coughed out before rebelling. A gust of wind ruffled the crest of the red pines rising on the hill behind us. The rectangular hay field spread like an apron at the base of the knoll. If the storm drenched the windrows before the hay was baled, the alfalfa would only be good for mulching fruit trees.

"Maybe the tension needs adjusting, like on my sewing machine," I said.

"Think we've got it." John slid out from under the baler. Hydraulic oil and grease streaked his blue shirt. "Hope the goats appreciate this."

Larry handed John a quart of lemonade. He chugged it, and wiped his mouth on his shirt collar. A silver Honda rolled up the driveway carrying Larry's wife, Jane. Another rumble of thunder.

"Baler broke." Larry said.

"What's new?" Jane pulled on her gloves.

"Ready to roll." John climbed onto his Ford tractor that pulled the baler. He revved the engine and pushed the power-take-off lever. The steel arms of the baler slammed in and out, feeding the maw a river of green. I mounted the Massy Ferguson pulling the hay wagon, shifted into second gear, and inched behind the baler. Jane brought bales to Larry who stacked them on the trailer.

Tree and barn swallows swooped and darted through the golden light of sunset, feasting on the insects disturbed from the windrows. A haze of dust drifted from behind the baler. Third cutting usually yields less hay than the earlier cuttings. At this point in the growing season, the soil was parched and needed rain, but not now. John skirted the edge of the pond and a pair of mallards splashed through the water as they flew off to a quiet spot in the bog.

Kajuga, Kajuga, thumped the baler. A wall of green rose behind me.

"Hey!" Larry shouted. "We're full."

Larry and I traded places. The toes of my boots found ledges in the scratchy cliff. Jane and I sprawled on the summit as the wagon rocked side to side. The sky was sinking into purple, and in the west Mercury stabbed a blade of silver. The tractor puttered the quarter mile to the hay barn built in the nineteenth century.

Knotholes had popped from the weathered siding, and some of the battens curled like tongues, allowing in slits of light. Once great Belgians with hooves like dinner plates had pulled hay from their mangers along the north wall. Leather halters with buckles had hung on the forged nails pounded into the beams. A couple of steel stanchions had also dangled against the wall before the barn had been remodeled for storing hay. Only a single horseshoe, wedged into a crack between an upright beam and angle brace, spoke of the barn's past glory.

Thick two-by-eight and two-by-ten boards had been nailed down where the horses and cows had bedded. Stacks of first and second cutting bales covered the deck. Larry drove the tractor into the center aisle that divided the barn in half. The wings of barn swallows sliced the air as the birds abandoned their nests anchored to the overhead beams. A loft holding bales of straw ran the width of the north side. Jane and I climbed down and tied bandanas over our noses.

"We'll toss; you stack," Larry said.

Jane and I carried the bales, and stacked them in a corner

where salt dusted the wooden planks. We placed the bottom tier with the stem side of the bale facing up, so that any moisture left in the hay would be wicked out. The other layers were stacked with the baling twine on top. Dust and bits of alfalfa leaves stung our eyes and clung to our sweat coated arms. Jane wore long sleeves, but the sharp ended stalks scraped my bare forearms. No wind stirred the air in the barn, still hot from hours of sunshine. Heat radiated from the fresh bales. Sweat coursed down my backbone and puddled above my collarbones. Thunder rumbled. Everyone's pace quickened.

"Good looking hay," Larry said and carried over the last two bales. "Hope John's about done baling."

Jane opened a thermos and we washed the chaff from our throats.

Heat lightning rippled across the western sky, illuminating the mass of thunderheads rising over the shoreline. After unloading the trailer we returned to the hay field. John leaned over the stalled baler. Alfalfa leaves coated the back of his blue shirt. Snarls of baling twine littered the ground.

"Can you see?" I offered him the silver thermos cap filled with lemonade. "Think we'll make it?"

"Barely." John downed the lemonade. "Better keep picking up. Try third low."

I eased the Massy Ferguson into third gear and flicked on the headlights. Wind swooshed through the pines, and patchy clouds scuttled overhead. Larry built another wall of bales. Suddenly, John closed the fins of the baler, jumped onto his tractor and roared over the windrows. The baler chewed and spat. A rain drop struck my cheek. Lightning ripped the darkening sky. Five seconds later, thunder answered. For centuries, farmers have gambled, waging against frost, drought, insects and spoiled hay. Another raindrop wet the steering wheel, then another. A dozen bales later, John cut the power-take-off shaft, parked his tractor, and covered the baler with a blue tarp. He heaved two bales at a time onto the hay wagon until the last ones were loaded.

"Move over." He nudged me onto the tractor's fender. My fingers gripped the steel as he shifted into high gear and raced towards the barn. Thunder vibrated through my metal seat. Rain streaked the dust from my face. Jane and Larry rolled behind in their car. We pulled into the barn, and rain beat the metal roof. Lightning flashed, striking something.

"That one was close," Larry said. "Think they'll mold?"

John slid a hand into a bale. "Still cool. We'll give them some space."

After we finished unloading, Jane and I stood in the doorway. Water sluiced off the roof and gouged a deeper trough along the drip line. Mist swept over us. We held our bandanas in the stream and washed our faces and necks. The guys joined us.

"Too bad about the rest," Jane said.

"We need the rain," John said.

"Good color to the alfalfa," Larry said.

"Yeah, hope the goats appreciate it," John answered.

In late December, our gray tabby Spencer huddled on the milking stanchion, his fur puffed against the cold, waiting for me to fill his milk bowl. Shawls of cobwebs draped the fly speckled windows and beams. Two brown and white faces peered over the top boards of the stalls, eager for their dinner. Rosemary jumped onto the stanchion, and I pressed my scarf swathed head against her belly. We drew heat from each other. As she relaxed, her milk descended, and my fingers closed over her teats. Like the roll of a rocking chair, the steady motion removed from my mind the images of dry irrigation ditches and diseased blueberry canes. The rhythm cultivated a daydream of peach trees loaded with blushing fruit. Rosemary's teeth crunched corn, while Poppy snuffled in their manger for a tidbit of alfalfa. As the foam rose in the milk bucket, so did the barometer of my heart. I filled Spencer's bowl with milk and set it on a sill beam. His pink tongue flicked in and out. I studied Rosemary's expanding girth, humbled by my dependence upon her to provide both milk and fertilizer for my garden. Spencer vibrated beneath my hand as I pet him.

"Enjoy. It's the last night for milking until kidding time." I turned off the lantern.

As kidding time approached, I checked the goats four or five times a day. Supposedly, when the Rosemary's spine straightened, the babies were moving into the birthing position. I had scribbled dates on the calendar five months ago when she was bred, but nature would have her way. My birthing kit sat on the kitchen counter with sewing thread, shears and iodine. Rosemary sprawled in the slanted afternoon sunshine, her rounded white belly quivered when a kid kicked. John and I leaned over the paddock fence, calculating.

"So when do you think they'll kid?" I asked. "I say Valentines Day."

"Probably later. Doesn't your book say that goats choose the nastiest day? It'll probably be blowing and sleeting."

But sun and a southern breeze warmed the shed when I spied Rosemary pawing the straw into a nest. I dashed to the house for my book and midwifery supplies. Rosemary moaned when I sat next to her. Our golden-green eyes met. Pain swam in her pupils, thin wafers of black mica.

"You're doing fine." I glanced at my pocket watch. After the first kid arrived, any other kids should follow within the next thirty or forty minutes, unless Rosemary was having a difficult birth. Then I would call a vet to stick his hand inside her womb and search for dead kids; I prayed that the vet could stay home.

Rosemary groaned, and her back arched. She strained, and relaxed as the contraction subsided. She rested her head on my lap, and I stroked her chin. When she tensed again, I dug my feet into the straw. From down in the bog, the spring peepers chanted, and I heard John on his tractor, mowing brush in the blueberries.

"Soon this will be over." I scratched between her ears. Yet, how much longer could she last? Rosemary whimpered and squeezed her eyes. I gritted my teeth. She bawled and stood up.

Two ebony hooves inched out of her rear end. A pink nose slid towards me.

"It's coming! Push!"

Rosemary bawled, again. Her body stiffened in the contraction. The embryonic sac split as it struck against the straw. The kid sneezed. Rosemary turned, nuzzling and greeting her newborn while I cleared the mucus away from his pink nose. The baby mewed as Rosemary licked away the bloody slime; her rough tongue massaged his muscles as she cleaned him. I rubbed a soft towel over the gangly kid who sat head erect, calling to his mother.

I scanned Rosemary's belly. A hollow whittled one side, but on the other side, a bump told me that another kid traveled towards daylight. Rosemary shuddered. Backing up, she sank onto the straw. I bundled baby number one in a towel and moved him out of her way. Her muscles quivered. She groaned and pushed.

Two kids dove out, struggling in their embryonic sac. I broke the membrane; blood and fluid gushed. The tiny kids bleated, and Rosemary's tongue scrubbed them. Now and then, she paused to drink from a bucket of warm water sweetened with molasses that would give her energy and minerals. The twins shook their ears and cocked their heads when they heard baby number one bleating. Poppy stuck her head above the boards of the stall, eying the newcomers. Spencer paced on the stanchion, eager for the first drops of milk. The tractor stopped in the farmyard. A few minutes later, John pulled open the barn door.

"How many?" he asked, rubbing Spencer's back.

"Three. Why don't you help me tie off their cords? The first one's been trying to nurse."

John held each baby on its back while I slipped sewing thread around the cord, dabbed iodine, and clipped off the string of flesh that could wick infection into the navel. Rosemary nuzzled each kid as we placed them back with her.

"Two girls and a boy," John said. Spencer rubbed against his legs. "I'll milk while you fetch the bottles. With three trying to nurse, we better make sure they each drink some colostrum."

We filled the bottles. Less than an hour old, yet the three kids tottered about the stall. We cupped their faces in our hands, and guided the rubber nipples into their mouths. I felt the kid's heart fluttering.

"We should let them nurse for a day or two," I said. "Then bottle feed them."

"Yes, but a little snack from a bottle will help them bond with us." John cuddled a kid. "And will make the transition easier."

Rosemary licked the milk from her kids' chins as they snuggled for a nap. We heard licking and spied Spencer with his head in the milk bucket.

"Fat cat." John picked him up.

"Next time, remember the lid." I peered into the bucket.

During their first week, I found the babies breathing as one mass of white and brown heaped in a cubby formed from two bales of straw. But after two weeks, when John and I arrived with a bucket of filled milk bottles, I heard the kids careening off the walls of their stall. They dashed up to us, butting our legs; their lips nursed my apron as we aimed bottles into the snarl of bodies. The sound of sucking swept away their cries of hunger.

Once the bottles emptied, the kids danced on their back legs, their front hooves drumming the stall's door. When I unlatched it, the babies exploded out of the barn. Leaping, gyrating, they raced and gamboled. Spencer contemplated their antics. Spring fever dissolved his sloth, and he darted up a nearby pin oak.

I skipped around the picnic table, and my corps de ballet chased me. A little buck jumped onto the table and tap danced. Suddenly, like a flock of swallows, they swooped off the table and across the lawn. One nipped a daffodil. Another broke a lilac branch.

"Stop that! Recess is over," I called, but no one paid attention.

John scooped up two squirming kids, while I captured the third culprit. We shut them in the paddock and latched the gate.

"It was a good idea to turn this into an animal barn," John said, and eyed the back wall. "I could build an addition on the back for a large stall."

"For more goats?"

"No, for a team of oxen."

BETWEEN THE LEAVES

"The farmer waits for the precious produce of the soil, being patient for it." James 5:7

The grass scrunched beneath our boots one early June morning, as John and I eyed the frost damage in our blueberry fields. Although our fruit farm hugged the eastern shore of Lake Michigan, the rippling mass of water had not warmed last night's air, protecting our blooming bushes from the frigid temperatures tumbling south from Canada.

"Twenty-seven degrees," John said. "We lost most of the crop. Maybe we need to diversify."

"What did you have in mind?"

"Peaches. We'll try some early varieties that we can harvest before our blueberries ripen, plus Red Havens. Everyone wants those."

I could see the swirl of orange and yellow blending through the fuzzy skin and could taste the juice oozing from sun-colored flesh. John knew peaches were my favorite fruit, but he had grown up on this farm and understood what he was proposing, while I had no inkling of what raising peaches would demand from me.

We sent in our nursery order. A year later, we squatted at the edge of a sandy field, and uncovered the peach saplings from their sphagnum moss nest. Yesterday, we had pounded a grid of stakes into the soil to show where to plant the trees. At the bottom of the hill, the warp of blueberry rows spread across the bog. I positioned a whip.

"Another inch over," John shouted.

I moved the sapling, and heeled it in with my boot, hoping I had hit the correct spot, but knowing that John would probably alter the location.

"It's leaning the wrong way." John jogged over. "Because the prevailing winds come from the southwest, you lean the tree a bit that way, then the constant wind pressure will straighten it." He tipped the tree slightly, and pressed the soil with his large palms. "Like that," he added.

I had noticed how old fruit trees slanted eastward, as if someone had combed their branches and aimed them in one direction. But I had never thought how the breath of Lake Michigan shaped the orchards.

All morning, I pulled trees from a bucket filled with a murky concoction smelling of seaweed and fish emulsion. I patted them into their new home, and John called out how to shift the sapling a wee bit to align the row perfectly. Maybe husbands and wives shouldn't work together day after day, I mused. Yet, I had farmed long enough to understand that in the future when John sprayed or planted cover crops, he would need to pass between straight rows of trees. Planting an orchard required the same precision as when I pieced a quilt, where a slight deviation in block size can pucker seams when the blocks are sewn together. And unlike corn or soybean farmers, we were investing in a crop that should produce for fifteen or more years. If the rows wandered, we would wrestle with our mistakes for two decades.

Over the next three years, the orchard grew. Each April, I ducked my head between limbs that clawed at my hair and squinted into the web of twigs. Which ones should I cut? John sawed larger branches, molding the tree into a bowl-shape, so the limbs would curve outward to capture sunshine. I snipped suckers to allow for good airflow between the leaves. Even if subzero temperatures withered the buds in January or February, a fruit farmer must perform this ritual although he knows that there will be no harvest in August. Throughout the summer, John would rumble between the trees, disking, spewing seaweed sprays and spreading organic fertilizers. The first year, a few pink stars shimmered on our infant trees, but we plucked them off so that the trees would concentrate on growing. Like parents eager for a baby to lift her foot and reach for that first step, we had to wait two to three years before we could pick fruit from our orchard. We learned to gaze beyond the immediate, and to look back at those who planted these fields before us.

John and I were not the first farmers to plant peaches on that glacial moraine whose height would protect our trees from frost. In 1837, when James McCormick settled the farm that John's grandfather later bought, McCormick and other pioneer families set out a few peach trees along split rail fences and grew enough fruit for their families. But in 1870, McCormick and two other farmers listened to men near Benton Harbor brag about the profits they harvested from their peach orchards. One Berrien county farmer had earned over $1,500 by shipping his crop to Chicago. McCormick returned to Fennville, sifted the sandy loam through his fingers and recognized the potential for raising peaches. In 1872, he and his friends each set out 1,000 peach trees. The secluded landscape protected the orchard from pests and blights that proliferated in densely settled fruit regions. By the late 1870's, McCormick heaped baskets of blushing peaches onto his buckboard, and drove his team three miles north to the Kalamazoo River where he unloaded his crop onto a boat that floated down to Saugatuck. McCormick's fruit was combined with thousands of baskets of peaches that filled schooners and steamships that traveled across Lake Michigan.

Peaches provided the cash for McCormick to expand his farm. He had previously replaced his log cabin with a clapboard house, now he constructed new barns. As other families moved to the lakeshore, they planted peaches. Rows of slate-colored branches and glossy serrated leaves dipped and ascended the five miles of land sweeping towards Lake Michigan. Acres of rosy blossoms foamed over the hills. More white farmhouses with wide front porches dotted the main road, and witnessed to the bounty sailing away from the docks at Pier Cove and Saugatuck. Each day during the harvest season, two ships headed to Chicago, while two others glided towards Milwaukee.

In 1880, a fungus that government pathologists named the "peach yellows" erupted in the orchards. Decades later, scientists would identify the "yellows" as a phytoplasma disease caused by a group of organisms similar to viruses with the characteristics of bacteria. The nineteenth century farmers spied the odd peaches ripening earlier than the main crop; peaches streaked with red that ran from the pit and through the sweet flesh. On the same limb, new sprouts with yellow leaves transferred the disease to existing branches. Foliage withered. Flabby yellow leaves littered the ground beneath naked trees, and stuck to the toes of damp work boots as the farmers waded through their orchards.

Communities appointed "yellow commissioners" to inspect orchards and to eradicate diseased trees. Axes thudded. Oxen bawled as they leaned into their yokes and ripped roots from the earth. Those who refused to topple their trees witnessed the commissioners ordering other men to chop, and the officials added the cost of the removal onto the farmer's taxes.

A few years later, the "little peach", another phytoplasma disease ravaged the orchards. Instead of swelling into honey sweet fruit, the marble-size peaches clung to the limbs. Axes flashed again. Orchards shrank. The scarred patches of land lay fallow. Some farmers plowed up pastures and planted new peach orchards, others set out cherry or pear orchards.

The winter of 1899 blew arctic air across the Lake Michigan. Temperatures plunged below zero. Peach trees split. Buds and limbs froze. Most farmers chopped down the last of their trees. And the few that gritted their teeth and replanted, lost again on October 6th, 1906 when they awoke to a temperature of six degrees. Ninety percent of the orchards from the Indiana/Michigan border to Traverse City died that night. Many bankrupt families left the area or plowed their fields for corn. The tenacious tore out their trees and replanted.

Yet, even today, orchards are still butchered. Instead of axes, bulldozers with steel teeth grab at the peach, apple, and pear trees and rip them from neighboring farms. They roar over to a brush pile and toss away those years of pruning, spraying, and cultivating. The perfume of apples no longer scents the air, nor do clouds of pear blossoms drift across the hills in May. After the spring rains, thin gray tendrils of smoke smudge the sky as fruit farmers burn brush piles filled with dead trees. The men all say the same things.

"Too much work. The fruit canners barely paid me what I spent on spray and fuel for the tractors. Guess we'll rent the land for corn."

John and I mourned over the corn stubble that replaced the orchards, but we understood the economic struggles that squeezed the aging farmers into life-changing decisions. Our future would be different, we promised each other. While our neighbors contended with the local fruit cannery's politics, like James McCormick we would send our peaches and blueberries to Chicago, Milwaukee and Minneapolis. We would seek out the budding organic markets.

One evening in the third spring, we ambled through our orchard. The hum of bees' wings vibrated in the soft air. From the sugar bush to the west, the voice of a thrush melted over us.

"The *Lorings* have the showiest bloom." John pulled a flower the color of strawberries and cream from a twig and checked the stamen. "Looks like the bees have been working. We'll have lots to thin come June."

"Thin about a hand-length apart," John spread his thick and calloused fingers along the peach branch. He glanced at my smaller palm. "Maybe for you, one-and-a-half-hands." His blue shirt matched the cloudless sky where the faint face of the moon slid westward. Only eight in the morning, and already I tasted the salt beading above my lips.

"When I was little, but then you never grew beyond little," John stretched his long arms and grasped an upper limb, "we used to have green peach fights" He lobbed a fuzzy marble at me.

"Very funny. Quit it, if you want my help." I tugged off tiny green peaches and dropped them. The fourteen inches that separated my height from the top of John's head relegated my hands to the limbs nearer the ground. A few rubbery dandelion stems protruded from leaves flattened by lack of rain, but like farmers' feet, their taproots sank deep into the soil.

"You can leave a few clusters," John instructed. "But we don't want to overburden the branches with too much weight. And we want big peaches."

My hands and wrists itched as peach fuzz sifted into my pores. A line from Elinor Wylie's poem *Wild Peaches* taunted me: "We'll live among wild peach trees, miles from town." I wondered if Miss Wylie had thinned peaches.

All week long, the deer flies buzzed my face and peach fuzz

prickled my neck. My feet stumbled on the peaches littering the earth. I counted off the remaining trees while John stomped down the rows, heaved a ladder against a sturdy branch, and ripped off peaches. For him, we were repeating a paradigm established in his youth, while I still measured each breadth with my hand and analyzed my work. But I had discovered that the rhythms of the seasons would rescue me; just as I reached a saturation point and wanted to never thin another peach tree, we finished. The pattern shifted to cutting hay and harvesting early blueberries.

On a scorching August afternoon, I leaned against the tailgate of our pick-up and splashed ice water over my face. The green marbles had expanded into baseball-size globes streaked with rouge. Thick fuzz covered the swollen golden cheeks. My eyes itched, my nose burned, and fur coated my cracked lips. Why hadn't we planted u-pick apples or pumpkins? All morning we had picked bushels of peaches, only to realize that in the extreme heat, the fruit was ripening faster than we could pick it.

John capped the thermos and smiled. "No way to avoid this. Just have to get the job over. Here." He held up my picking bag. I slipped my arms into the harness and settled the straps over my shoulders. The metal bin with a canvas bag attached at the bottom would hold a half-bushel of peaches. When full, I would position it over a plastic container, unhook the latches that closed the bag, and fruit would flow out the opening.

"I'll take these two rows, you head down that one. Remember, rounded fruit, ripe yet firm," John said.

Yellow jackets and wasps strolled across the fruit. I scanned each peach before twisting it off the branch and placing it in my bag. If I squeezed the peach, the flesh would bruise and sell at a lower price. The weight of the picking bag pulled at my shoulders. The dense foliage trapped the humidity. Sweat soaked my shirt and rolled down my backbone. Peach fuzz continued to sift over me until a mud of sweat and fuzz plastered my bare arms and neck. We should have worn long sleeves, but at ninety-eight degrees, John and I had reckoned we would rather itch than drop from heat exhaustion.

While I filled one lug, John filled three. I pretended we were in a blizzard, imagining snowdrifts shifting between the rows, but only heat waves shimmered. The white flakes fluttering were the buckwheat flowers that escaped John's disk when he plowed down the cover crop. I finished my row and trudged over to where John labored

"Only six more," John said. He stripped peaches with both hands and the sagging branch sprang upward.

Five, four, I counted off the trees as I picked. Like the branches released from their burden of fruit, I felt the load lift. We opened our picking sacks and the last peaches slumped into the lugs.

"We'll unload and head to the lake," John said between swallows of ice water. "Not too much brown rot considering the heat and humidity. Guess I sprayed enough sulfur to stop it."

How can he care about such details, when my mind was fried? I hung my head out the pick-up window, relishing the rush of air.

We waved as John's father drove by us on a tractor, his baseball cap shading his bald head. We pulled into a metal pole building on my in-laws' farm. A thin man with a goatee and a strawberry blonde ponytail dumped blueberries into an aluminum hopper. He whacked it, and berries tumbled out and onto a conveyor belt. Motors growled as the belt rolled between a half-dozen men and women whose fingers plucked out green berries and stems. The tangy scent of fermented berries and peaches rose from unwashed lugs still sticky with juice. I plodded through the shed while John started up the forklift. Two Latino women sorted peaches picked from John's folks' orchards.

"*Hola*," one of the women said, her coffee-colored hands continuing to roll fruit as she inspected them for blemishes. Her pink t-shirt announced that *Virginia is for lovers,* and stretched over her hips that jiggled beneath blue polyester pants.

"*Buenos días.*" I watched her hands flit like sparrows, the same strong hands that probably slapped out two-dozen tortillas before the sun rose.

"*Caliente, sí?*" the other woman asked. Her eyes showed gratitude for an inside job. Sweat glistened about her hairline. A man's white long sleeve dress shirt protected her amber skin from the fuzz, and its hem dropped below the waist of her brown skirt. Like her co-worker, she stood in gray sneakers, ankles puffy from the heat.

"*Sí, mucho caliente.*" I answered.

Hearing the squeal and grind of the folklift's brakes, I climbed back onto the pick-up and heaved lugs onto the tailgate. John stacked them onto a wooden pallet. Stooping over, I spied a couple in their mid-thirties standing in the doorway that connects the packing shed with the fruit stand. Her spotless T-shirt skimmed linen slacks and the crease still ran down the man's short-sleeved shirt. They could have been any of our professional friends from a nearby college or business, but the cut of their clothing spoke of Chicago.

For an instant, I saw myself as an eight-year-old with pigtails. I had held my father's hand as we had watched farmers sort apples in shed near a fruit stand. A gray-haired man in a denim jacket had smiled, paused, and placed a Spy in my palm.

"Enjoy," he had said and walked back to his bin of apples.

Now, I dragged a stack of lugs towards the tailgate while glancing at the couple whose eyes followed our arms. Many cars parked along Lakeshore Road sported Illinois license plates, and I did not begrudge them their Michigan sanctuary. If I lived where the black- top sucked up heat during the day and spat it back at night, I would yearn to escape from diesel fumes and the smell of tar. Like the nineteenth century urban denizens who bought McCormick's peaches, these folk stuffed boxes of fruit into their car trunks and blessed me with an income.

But what would it be like to spend a muggy August afternoon driving to antique shops instead of scratching my skin off? Or sharing a picnic on a screened-in porch of a summer cottage before stretching out in a hammock with a book? We could have been them, I reminded myself. After college, we could have earned more initials to tack behind our names and worked for a petroleum company or spent our summers creating syllabuses for our fall classes. I could be wearing sandals and choosing a quart of peaches at a fruit stand, but they wouldn't taste the same.

Despite the ache from where the picking bag straps had dug

into my shoulders, only an hour ago, I had stood in air thick with the perfume of peaches and picked a hidden treasure that our hands had missed the day before.

My fingers dimpled the flesh, soft as sponge cake. I stripped the skin with my teeth, pulling off patches, and revealing a sunset beaded with sugar. Juice sluiced down my elbows. My tongue danced with the flesh as it dissolved into honey. Bite by bite, I swallowed pink flowers, an amber sunset, and the hum of bees before I tossed the pit to the chipmunks, and licked my fingers.

I studied the fuzz lodged in the creases of my work boots and picked up two lugs. I was the keeper of such riches.

"Don't hurt your back," John said. His soaked shirt clung to his back.

"I want to get this over." I licked fuzz from my lips. I could hear the waves of Lake Michigan sucking at the pebbles, calling me.

We pulled into the public beach at Pier Cove; threw down our towels and raced across the burning sand. Just before we plunged into the silver-blue water, I noticed the same couple sitting on a bench, gazing at the horizon, uninterested in diving into the Lake that they admired. John and I lunged beneath the waves. Cold water drained the heat hazing my brain. The waves lapped at the layers of sweat and fuzz.

I scrubbed my arms, neck and scalp. My muscles relaxed, and my heartbeat slowed. I scanned the narrow strand where a score of mothers sat on beach towels chatting with each other. They watched their children duck in and out of the waves. A few elderly couples in straw hats lounged on deck chairs, reading. Only white skin shimmered in the heat waves rippling off the sand. What a different scene from the evenings when the migrant families stomped and splashed on the shore. Like us, they spent their daylight hours in the fields and arrived at sunset to cool their swollen feet. Fathers tossed their children in the waves while mothers stood on the strand in drenched skirts, cuddling infants.

Eyes closed, I drifted on my back. Liquid arms rocked me. Tomorrow I would pack blueberries in the shade, slapping cellophane wrappers and rubber bands onto pints of berries. The next day we would pick peaches again. More sweat and fuzz. A slightly larger wave nudged me towards the shore. Yet, somewhere between drooping leaves, I would find another peach to savor, a priceless gift waiting for my hands.

PULLING TOGETHER

"Two are better than one because they
have a good return for their labor...
A cord of three strands is not easily broken."
Ecclesiastes 5:9, 12

John set down the hand-hewn beam, penciled two lines near one end, and swiped his chainsaw along his marks. Sawdust spattered and filled the nicks left by the nineteenth century man who shaped the beam with adze and broad axe. The settler had gained his skills from his father and friends, while we learned from his handiwork.

"Chip away on either side of the cut marks." John handed me a chisel and a mallet made from a four-by-four chunk attached to a wooden handle. "Make the tenon look like a tongue."

Kneeling beside the beam, I whacked at the chisel and flakes of wood curled off, exposing gold against the aged gray. Although I had helped my father with various woodworking projects, John and I had never studied timber framing. We were young and cocksure, believing that hard work and a sense of vision could erect a barn.

"What kind of wood is this?" I asked.

"Most of the beams are spruce and white pine, plus a few oak. You'll know those when you find them." A straw hat shaded John's fair skin and hid his face as he plopped another beam into place and repeated the saw cuts.

I hammered and tapped; carving a tenon that would fit into a mortise, a hole dug into another beam. Who had lifted his ax, cut this pine tree, and shaped it into a barn beam? Was he a Dutchman like my husband or a Scotsman driven from his native land? When he had swung his axe, had he dreamt of a shelter for his team of oxen, and a loft where his children could play on rainy days? Straddling the timber, I chipped away, aware of the dozens of beams waiting.

We had gathered the lumber from neglected barns filled with the traces of nineteenth century glory. Rusted horseshoes, rectangular metal stanchions for milking cows, worn and moldy leather harnesses and rotting straw. The timbers whispered of a time when a day began and ended by filling buckets with milk. Large hands had folded over small ones as children learned to milk or curry horses. The daily labors had linked fathers and sons, mothers and daughters who had learned to work together. But those lives had sifted into the soil and only the barns remained. High winds off of Lake Michigan had lifted a few shingles from the barns' roofs; rain had seeped into the mortises; rot had crept along the beams. Rafters had sagged and collapsed. As the sashes had decayed, windowpanes had crashed onto the ground. Starlings had built nests, a sign of the building's demise.

Along with our friend, Larry, our hands had dismantled timbers. We pried out square iron nails with wrecking bars, and collected them in the front pockets of our overalls. Like a biologist dissecting a frog, we studied the slope of the angle braces, the thickness of the weight bearing timbers, and the spacing of the upright beams. The barns were our textbook. We took our notes from the wood.

After studying the designs in Eric Sloane's book *An Age of Barns*, John and I had drawn plans for a bank barn built into the north side of Pleasant Hill with a canti-levered second story, where underneath it we could pull a wagon load of hay out of a shower or store equipment. The fall before our barn raising a local firm poured the footings, a retaining wall, and a cement cave that would serve as a future root cellar. Later, we would extend the retaining wall by building wings with field stone to further stabilize the hill.

Midsummer dawned soft with a sky as blue as chicory flowers. Only a breeze licked the tops of the red pines as dozens of cars and trucks parked along the edges of our cherry orchard. Some folks had driven two hours to attend the barn raising. Some John and I had never met, but were friends of friends who had learned of the event and asked if they could come. We gleaned people from our church, food coop, and organic farming organization, plus musicians and contra-dancing friends. Teachers, actors, retired folks, homemakers, soft hands and calloused hands, they drifted about the barn site in their overalls and jeans. Toddlers and children sensed the adults' excitement and chased each other up and down the sandy hill. Only the dozen carpenters wearing their scarred leather tool belts had any idea of *what* we were about to do, and even most of them had never raised a timber-framed barn. Five score strong, the crowd inspected the grid work of beams spread out like the flaps on a box. For the past month, John, our friend, Larry, and I had eyed the bubble on our levels as we shimmed and teased the timbers into the bones of a barn. Now, wearing a T-shirt and jeans, Larry stood next to John.

"Everyone listen," John called. Bearded, in a blue shirt, broadfall pants, and straw hat, John looked like an old timey preacher, gathering a flock together to for baptism.

"Remember, everyone's lives are more important than this barn," John said. "If anything starts to fall, get out of the way. Watch out for the guy next to you. We're going to start with the shortest section and learn as we go."

John positioned men with poles on one side a section of linked beams, a header with two uprights. Other folks grabbed the ropes attached to the header and lined up on the side opposite. Like dancers coupled for the Virginia Reel, we waited for the call.

"Heave ho!" John shouted and the men pushed against their poles, lifting the header inches off the ground.

Hand over hand; we strained on the thick rope, tightening the line. Our row of people moved backward as the men with the poles crept forward. The scent of hemp and grease rose from the rope moving beneath my gloves. All eyes stared as the giant black jaw opened against the blue.

"Watch it!" John yelled. "It's twisting. Bring it down."

"Ease up on the ropes," our friend, Larry shouted. "Easy, not too fast."

"What's wrong?" a friend asked.

"I don't know," I answered.

The jaw closed. A covey of carpenters flocked about the section, tightening bolts, scanning their levels, checking the angle braces that ran at a 45-degree angle from the uprights to the header. We had waded into the past, dipped our toes into current, but none of us knew how to swim.

"Positions!" John called.

We resumed our dance, hoping and praying that this time we would succeed. Mouths set; shoulders stiff. We glanced at each other.

"Push! Pull!" John called.

Inch by inch we took in rope. Teeth clenched, we dug the heels of our boots into the sand and defied gravity.

"It's working!" Deborah shouted.

The header sliced the sky. Sunlight flashed on the steel bolts. John and Larry grabbed two by fours and nailed them to the sill plate and uprights in order to stabilize the section. Everyone cheered.

"Perfect!" Someone shouted.

"Gotta scab one on higher," John called. He pulled himself up onto a stringer, curled his legs around an upright and shimmed skyward; denim and leather scraped wood until his hat brushed the header. Larry lifted one end of long two by eight into John's hands and anchored the other end to the sill.

Deborah positioned her camera and clicked the shutter. "What a moment."

"Think we'll finish the whole barn like the Amish do?" a woman I didn't know asked. "Roof and all?"

"Probably not," I replied. "But we hope to get all the beams up. Thanks for helping. We need everyone."

In many small towns or segments of blocks in cities, the nuts and bolts of neighboring are not entirely lost, but usually sports teams or man-made festivals link the neighbors and not the interdependence of sharing agrarian labors. We who joined hands that mid-summer day recognized the satisfaction of unified strength aimed at a common purpose.

The sun arced across the sky. In between raising and securing the assembled beams, clusters of women pulled nails from salvaged two by eight boards, content to work in the shade. Chatter mixed with laughter, shouting and the whack of hammers. Four children played with scraps of lumber beneath a pin oak. Their hands built a barn in less than an hour, and their toy tractors rumbled through the sand. None of the preschoolers lived on farms, but their imagination dwelled in the spirit of the moment as their parents sculpted memories.

Section by section we erected the ribs of the barn. Each section contained a longer header, included more upright beams and was heavier. But the repetition of the process trained our eyes and hands. Slivers, blisters became badges. Finally, we stared at a seventy-two-foot section weighing three tons. The golden light of evening cast long shadows. To the west, apricot and lavender shimmered through the leafy canopy of the cherry orchard. Dirt smudged our cheeks, sunburn reddened our necks and arms, and three-corner tears dimpled a few jeans. The ranks had dwindled to three score.

"This is it." John looked about. "It'll take all we've got to get this one up."

"We can do it!" A friend shouted.

A line of men gripped poles and poked the giant sprawled beside the footings. John and Larry exchanged glances. On the other side of the leviathan, hands gripped ropes.

"HEAVE!" the men yelled.

An inch, a foot higher, the beams creaked. Faces grew red. Our arms quivered. Like a squall line lifting across the lakeshore, the timbers crept across the sky.

"Tighten those ropes!" Larry shouted.

"Mark, Dave…" John called out a dozen names. "Drop your poles and hit the ropes!" A groan rippled over the remaining men holding poles as the carpenters scrambled for the ropes.

"HURRY!" one of the men said as he leaned into his pole. "Can't hold much longer."

Rope slid through our fingers as many hands drew the timbers perpendicular. John and Larry slapped two by four braces into place. Tears glistened in the eyes of a fellow wearing a red bandana headband whom I had not met before today.

"It's so beautiful," he said. "I never dreamed I'd be part of something like this."

"Thought I was going to collapse," another man said. His white painter's overalls covered his round body.

"Photo shoot!" Deborah called. "Everyone up, like in those old photos."

"But this one will have women in it," Mary said as she climbed up the framework.

The nimblest balanced on the upper beams, straddling the header. Parents placed their sons and daughters on the lower stringers, and curled an arm about their children. The rest of us scampered for safe places where we lounged against uprights or leaned against stringers. Like a wedding photo, the shutter marked a commencement of traditions and community.

"Good thing you chose the longest day," Larry said. "Took all day."

"Yeah, but what a day," Deborah said.

Twenty-five years later on mid-summer's eve, many of the same hands spread their snapshots across our picnic table. The day of the barn raising has been retold over the years and has expanded into a mythical tale. We had discovered unity through timber-framing, from creating a space of our own. The board and batten walls and tin roof have sheltered baby showers, weddings and summer solstice parties. This evening, rows of casseroles line a trestle table constructed from rough sawn boards and sawhorses, and a yeasty fragrance floats from baskets of bread. New friends scan the photos and ask questions. Our children chase their own wee ones. Holding glasses of wine or punch, we bend our graying heads over the photos; some of us pull out reading glasses. The images of the barn raising mingle with the celebrations that emerged over the following years.

Those who gathered that evening had gripped each other's

hands even more tightly through deaths, surgeries, and divorces, the struggles that divide life from life. Some folk had splintered away, but we still spoke of them when telling stories. Between these beams, we encouraged each other and new friends to grab hold of the ropes and pull together.

GRAFTED

One January morning, John and I sat in a Colombian orphanage squirming on plastic chairs while the director gathered our soon-to-be sons. We knew that this moment would change our lives forever; still we embraced visions of picking peaches together and fishing from our pond. Pinch faced children dressed in t-shirts and shorts or sleeveless dresses clustered about the doorway staring at us.

"*Yo también,*" they pleaded. "Take me, too."

Despite the kind caretakers, colorful posters, and pint-sized tables, and chairs, the wee ones' eyes yearned for someone to claim them as a son or daughter. While I longed to gather them into our home; the visas and paperwork sewn into my dress only offered passage for our sons.

Footsteps clicked down the hallway, parting the flock of children. Four-year-old Mathew clung to a worker's hand. The director carried a scrawny, twenty-month-old Carlos, and placed him in my arms. When Matthew climbed into John's lap, he appeared the size of a two-year-old. Carlos' bloated belly resembled the image of a child in a famine poster. The boys' hair hung limply and scabies dotted Matthew's skin. A year ago, our sons had lived on the streets of a barrio lined with sheet metal huts and garbage filled gutters, before their biological mother relinquished them. The anguish of abandonment still spilled from Matthew's eyes. He fiddled with John's wedding ring. Anxiety tumbled inside me. We knew how to nurture the orchards on our farm, but how could John and I heal these two shattered lives? We expressed our thanks, and said farewell to the orphanage staff. Our Colombian lawyer escorted us back to a boarding house in time for lunch.

A good meal would prove that the lads could trust us, I thought. But first, they needed to wash their hands.

"*Vamos a la comida,*" I told my new sons. "*Pero necessita lavar las manos.*"

"*NO,*" Matthew screamed. He collapsed, beating the bathroom floor and kicking me away.

Not a good beginning to parenthood. From the articles I had read, most families experienced a honeymoon period when yearning for adoptive parental approval, the newly grafted children behaved. Rebellion normally set in after two or three weeks, then the child determined to see what it would take for his new parents to reject him.

I leaned over to comfort Matthew. "*Por favor.*"

Whack! He beat me with his shoe until I took it from him. Matthew glared at me when I picked him up and carried him to lunch. The battles had begun.

That evening, I walked the hallways with a sobbing Carlos, his head on my shoulder. I rubbed his back, praying that gentle touches could communicate our love, but he continued to wail. Finally, I returned to our room and handed him to John.

"Your turn."

Instead of walking, John lay down on a bed and placed our son on his chest. Carlos whimpered, pressed his cheek against John and slept. I covered both of them with a small quilt I had brought, something comforting from our farm.

"Night." John closed his eyes.

On our last day in Bogotá, we strolled from the American Embassy with the boys' stamped papers tucked inside my dress. In twenty-four hours, our sons would walk upon the farm's soil and breathe Michigan air. When we passed a house with a garden enclosed by an iron fence, Carlos paused. He gripped the bars, studying the blooming plants and shrubs while Matthew ran down the sidewalk in pursuit of a motorcycle. John chased after him and snatched him from the street. Matt howled, sank to the sidewalk, and beat the cement in his third tantrum that morning. What had happened on those Colombian streets to ignite such rage? I prayed that the rhythms of farm life would provide Matthew the same peace that John and I cherished.

Carlos pointed his tiny finger at red blossoms.

"They're pretty aren't they? *Muy linda.* Your new home has lots of flowers...*muchas flores*," I said. "We'd better catch up." I scooped up Carlos, but he looked back, staring at the garden.

THE GREEN MAN

Spring refused to come one April. Beneath gray cirrus clouds, we worked with our ears hunched into the collars of our winter jackets. Seed packets waited to be planted, baby goats shivered, and the pastures remained dormant.

"Maybe instead of a summer solstice party, we should celebrate May Day," I said one evening.

"We'd have to hope for a warmer afternoon," John said.

"We need to call for Jack-in-the-Green. Beseech him to come and bring us spring."

"Who is that?" Carlos asked.

"Jack-in-the-Green is like the dryads in Narnia. The Green Man hides in the trees."

We lost something when we stopped listening to trees.

I called our friend, Brad who had built the sets and puppets for a national children's television program. Recently, he had moved out of New York City and into a log cabin surrounded by pines near the Lake Michigan shore. Now, he traveled the country, working for various theatres.

"Could you pin oak leaves to one of your puppets, dress him up as Jack-in-the-Green, so he could lead a May Day procession?" I asked.

"I think…I can come up with something better," Brad said. "I'll be down at the end of next week."

I sent out invitations: "Come call for Jack-in-the-Green!"

A week later, Brad, the boys, and I wandered in our woods. Brad's curly red hair sprung about his head; the wind reddened his freckled face. The cuffs of his flannel shirt peeked out from his winter jacket. Vines, as thick as my wrist, ascended ten feet from the earth, and snarled around an ash's lower limbs. We cut grape vines and looped the papery strands into coils. And from a nearby pond, we also gathered willow branches.

"What's Jack going to look like?" Carlos asked.

"Wait and see. I did a little research and found out what they did in England," Brad said.

Twelfth century Christianity embraced the Green Man as a symbol of regeneration and of the mysteries in creation. Throughout England, his stalwart head peered between hawthorn and oak leaves, embellishing chancels. His face was carved into the arches that supported churches, bringing the world of leaves and vines into worship. The mystic, Hildegarde of Bingen defined his spirit as *viriditas*, the greening of the soul. He is the essence of the woods, of hemlock needles brushing your face, and of tiny oak leaves telling you when to plant your garden. His scent is of leaf mold as when you pull back the leaves and find a morel mushroom. The wood thrush is his voice.

May Day morning, John and our friend, Deborah stapled dozens of multi-colored ribbons to a small pine tree we had cut for a May Pole. I carried a few peach branches flocked with pink flowers and whips of yellow forsythia blossoms to Brad. He had woven a wicker tube of willow and grape vines, and mounted it to a framework that would rest on his shoulders. A wicker head perched on the top of the tube. Connected to his body were thick sticks that formed long jointed arms, with roots lashed on as fingers. Grape vines, willow, sassafras and flowers held together by creativity and folklore.

"How can I help?"

"We need to weave the flowers into Jack's body. Save the peach blossoms for his head."

We wove the forsythia into a fringed skirt that kilted Jack's body and stuck the peach blossoms and dried wild oats into the top of Jack's head. Finally, Brad hid Jack in a small grove of pines near our animal barn.

One by one, the cars rolled up our driveway. Babies smiled from packs strapped onto their father's backs, grandmothers' clutched their sons' arms, and joined the waves of children climbing Pleasant Hill. They left their offerings for the potluck in the barn, and escaped outside to bask in the sunshine. In her long wool skirt, Deborah stood beating her bodhran.

"Come gather!" she called, the sleeves of her Gibson Girl blouse ballooning in the breeze. "We must find Jack-in-the-Green! He will whisper to the trees and bring forth leaves. He will lead us to the May Pole. But first we need music."

John slipped on his accordion while our friends, Barclay and Mark picked up their fiddles. Deborah handed out masks borrowed from Brad's costume trunks, and transformed the children into elves and trolls, woodland creatures with tall ears, tuffs of hair and large eyes.

"What shall we play?" John asked.

"*Harvest Home.*" Barclay played the opening notes.

The men headed the parade that skipped to the syncopated hornpipe, down Pleasant Hill, around the pond and towards the goat pasture.

"Where's Jack?" Deborah asked. "Can you see him?"

"He's not here!" the children shouted.

"We must call for him," Deborah said. "Repeat after me.

Jack-in-the-Green, Jack-in-the-Green,

Come out of the woods, where you may be seen!"

Nothing happened. A chicken squawked from the coop, and the goats lined up by the pasture fence and watched. The wind played in the silver maple tree standing at the edge of the pond.

"We must hold hands and say it louder," Deborah said.

Gathered in a ring, sopranos, alto, tenor and bass, the voices chanted along with Deborah. Slowly, pink flowers poked out from between pine branches. Jack emerged and stood on a small rise, a ten-foot tall puppet man. The children gasped.

"Jack, bring us spring!" Deborah called. "Help us celebrate the first of May."

Jack waved his arms, and the children rushed forward. Oversized boots protruded beneath a brown robe, but the wicker puppet concealed Brad's face.

"The May Pole, Jack, where did you hide it?" Deborah asked.

Jack bowed to the trees behind him. Three friends jogged over and hoisted the May Pole onto their shoulders. Like a flock of sparrows, the children escorted Jack who led the procession up Pleasant Hill, as fiddles and accordion played. Jack pointed a gnarled hand and the men sank the May Pole into a prepared hole. A south wind tossed the ribbons.

"Welcome spring!" Deborah called. "May our crops and gardens flourish. May the season be filled with good health and good friends. Let us dance!"

"Take a ribbon," I called. "One couple or person to a ribbon, facing another couple. We're going to duck and dive, like in a Kentucky running set. People on the inside go under the ribbon of the next person, then raise your ribbon and allow the progressing couple to go under yours."

Jack directed the musicians who lit into *On the Road to Boston*. Over, under, over, under, hands lifted pink ribbons, heads ducked beneath blue ribbons. We dipped back into traditions and dove into the present flow of the dance. Feet skipped, releasing the fragrance of the grass and damp soil. From their chairs, the older folks clapped along. Like the interlocking ribbons clothing the May Pole, we wound our lives together and wove joy into memories.

THE INDY POND RUNNERS

I am to blame for Carlos' love of ducks. He was five or six when we drove to the hatchery to pick up an order of chicks. Both boys peered at the aisles lined with incubators; the air vibrated with thousands of cheeping chicks. While I wrote out a check for our order, an older man stomped up and shouted over the cacophony.

"Would your sons like some ducks?"

Barely hearing, I nodded my head, and finished signing my check. Only when we started the drive home did I realize what I had done.

Ducks! Unlike chicks that gobble their food and snuggled in a fluffy heap, ducklings dabble in their water, drenching themselves, and everything nearby. And unless ducklings have a mother who rubs her own oil into their down, baby ducks chill easily and need human assistance. Raising ducklings meant more work for me.

After the ducklings gained feathers, Carlos begged to be their surrogate parent. He and his webbed-footed friends splashed together in a huge wash tub, or they followed him around, eating a trail of corn. Over the next couple of years, his enthusiasm for fowl flourished. He studied his copy of *Raising Poultry Successfully*, quoting passages that listed the ten important reasons why homesteads needed ducks. And he scanned poultry catalogs, memorizing breeds and duck trivia that he recited to me while I washed dishes. For his birthday we bought him Peking, Rouen and the diminutive English Call ducks, but our farm still lacked the upright Indian Runner breed.

One day, John arrived home from the feed mill with a scrap of paper bearing the phone number of someone selling runner ducks. Later that evening, we drove down that farm's lane, and spied a pen with dozens of quacking runner ducks.

"You can have the lot for twenty-five dollars," the woman offered.

John and I shook our heads. "Six," John said, "should be sufficient."

The boys dashed about the pen as the ducks wheeled in a great arc, swooping between their hands. Feathers swirled in tiny clouds. Again and again they circled and quacked, until at last the lads nabbed a half-dozen. We shut them into a large dog carrier, and once home, we deposited the ducks in their coop. The next morning, our sons opened the door and shooed out the Runners.

Only one duck ran for the pond, while the other five sped down the driveway. The boys pursued them, waving their arms; the ducks increased their speed and left behind two breathless boys.

"I guess that's the reason they're called runner ducks," John stated. "We'll never see them again."

Our sons hopped onto their mountain bikes and searched the farm. In the bog, I walked the miles of irrigation ditches, watching for a head to peek over a clump of quack grass. Nothing stirred. Come night time, the coyotes would feast on ducks. I gave up and decided to head out to the mail box. About a third of the way down our half-mile driveway, I spotted the tracks of webbed feet. The runners had made it that far before heading off for neighboring fields. Back at home, I found Carlos lettering out a reward notice: *Wanted alive, not dead, the Indy Pond Runners.* To assuage his grief, we returned to the duck farm and purchased five more ducks.

After residing in their new shelter for a couple of days, Carlos propped open the coop door, and allowed the ducks to exit as they willed. The lone runner from the first flock encouraged her friends to join her on the pond and away they paddled.

About a week later, I realized that I had not seen the runners that day. I strolled over to a where pines shelter a secluded section of our pond. The runners were dabbling and diving. I counted heads: one, two…five…seven…eleven! Our wayward ducks had snuck home.

The following morning, all the runners waited near the goat barn, quacking for corn. Carlos filled a small bucket and broadcasted the kernels around the barn yard. Out dashed the ducks. At last they had reached the finish line, and could partake of their homecoming breakfast at Carlos' feet.

PUMPKIN EATERS

After Carlos read Laura Ingalls Wilder's novel, *Farmer Boy*, he decided to emulate Almanzo Wilder and grow a giant pumpkin to enter in our local fair. We had encouraged both our sons to enjoy gardening, hoping that the past time might hold their interest in the years to come. Our eight-year-old sat at the kitchen table, his black-haired head bowed over seed catalogs, comparing different varieties. Finally, he selected one that had produced record breaking-pumpkins yet could be cultivated in the north.

In April, Carlos planted seeds in three peat pots, and examined them daily while waiting for them to sprout. As the earth shifted, the sun shone longer each day. The seedlings stretched thumb-size leaves that expanded into their true leaves. One late May afternoon, Carlos chose a location in our garden for his pumpkin patch. He set out the sturdy seedlings, and John showed him how to mulch the plants with a ring of compost. Over the summer months, the fertilizer would sift down through the humus as the plants' root systems expanded. Every day, Carlos dragged over the hose, and soaked the soil around the rambling plants.

When the pumpkins began to flower, Carlos snipped off all the blossoms from the largest plant, except for one yellow star-shaped flower that shone amidst the sea of mammoth leaves. By the Fourth of July, a small green globe had formed, and Carlos read to me the pages describing how Almanzo fed milk to his prize-winning pumpkin.

"Can we feed it some tonight?"

So that evening, Carlos carried a bowl of milk to his plants. We waded through the tangle of vines and leaves. He scooped a shallow depression in the mulch, and nestled in the bowl while I slit the underside of the vine near the small pumpkin. Here, he inserted a piece of string to serve as a wick that would dangle in the bowl and would drawn milk up into the stem. The next morning, Carlos inspected the bowl and reported that the level in it had not changed.

"It might take all day for the pumpkin to drink the milk," I said.

We checked that evening, but could only detect a slight difference. Come morning, the bowl lay upside down, and in the nearby corn patch, half eaten cobs littered the ground.

"Raccoons," Carlos said. "They ate the corn and drank the milk."

He refilled the bowl, but after another raccoon raid; he gave up. Carlos continued watering and mulching his plant, and out of the mass of leaves protruded a bulging green boulder. During August, yellow crept over the expanding pumpkin, and it darkened into a bright orange. Carlos filled out his entry form for the fair and on our evening strolls; we often ended up in the pumpkin patch estimating the behemoth's weight. Finally, fair week arrived in early September. John, Carlos, and I struggled to lift the monster into the back of our small station wagon.

"Must weigh at least two hundred pounds," John said.

We clambered aboard our sagging car, and headed to the fairgrounds. Unlike Almanzo's days, the judging would occur on the day before the fair opens, so we would not witness that exciting moment. One of the judges overseeing the vegetable exhibits greeted us at the entrance of the horticultural building where other folks' baskets of apples, green peppers, and tomatoes already decorated booths.

"Who raised this enormous pumpkin?" the man asked, as he and another fellow slipped a canvas sling beneath the beast.

"I did," Carlos answered.

"What's your secret?" the other judge asked. The men grunted as they lifted the sling, and lugged the giant over to where several other colossal pumpkins sat.

"Water and compost," Carlos said. "Sunshine and mulch."

"Good luck," the men called as we drove off.

Opening day arrived, and the oily fragrance of elephant ears drifted towards us as we raced by the Ferris Wheel, music blaring from the midway. We passed the stalls of sheep and hogs, aiming for the horticulture building. Carlos dashed to his pumpkin; its weight had been scratched into its thick rind.

"Two hundred and eighty-seven pounds!" he shouted. "But only second place." A red ribbon hung from the pumpkin's stem; next to it, another pumpkin wore the blue and boasted two hundred and ninety-five pounds.

"Winning second place is very good for your first try," John said, "It's an honor, too."

One of the judges ambled over and shook Carlos' hand. "Good work," the man said. "Don't give up. Enter again next year."

At the end of the fair, we trucked the pumpkin home, and shoved it next to a corn shock that decorated the garden shed. When the north wind swept the last of the gold and orange leaves from the sassafras trees near our house, we pondered what to do with Carlos' treasure? Considering all of his labors to grow the giant, we couldn't pitch the pumpkin into the compost.

"Cows think pumpkins are a special treat," Carlos said one morning. "We could feed my pumpkin to the oxen for Thanksgiving."

We rolled the pumpkin down to the oxen paddock, opened the gate, and heaved it in. The oxen strolled over and sniffed. Tolstoy chomped at a small split in the rind, and Leo gnawed into the orange flesh. All afternoon, the two of them cracked off chunks and masticated seeds, flesh and rind. That evening when we returned to the barn, the oxen's stomachs bulged, as they lounged in the paddock, chewing their cud. Only a few seeds sprinkled the ground; once again, Carlos' pumpkin had been a winner.

ELECTRICITY

"He rode upon a cherub and flew...
He sped upon the wings of the wind."
Psalm 18:10

Sweat oozed from every pore as I stared at the wooden plank ceiling, and yearned for enough electricity to turn a fan. Pine trees surrounded and smothered our timber-framed house. Having forsaken the even hotter loft where John snored, I smoothed my pallet of quilts on the downstairs rag rug, and reminded myself that many denizens of the world lived without electricity. We had willingly given away our toaster and blender, seeking the simpler life.

As a child, when I read the Laura Ingalls Wilder's books, her life sounded so romantic, reading by kerosene lamps, baking bread in a wood cook stove, milking a cow, and churning butter. My hands had worked at those chores today, and I had reaped a deep satisfaction. Yet, while my muscles could hoe cabbage, split kindling, and even pump a little water, I could not power a fan to shred the thick stillness.

In our dimly lit home, flashlights stood in the designated places on the kitchen counters; matches resided in a cubby formed by the beams slicing the wall behind the cook stove. Twice a week during the winter, I washed the glass globes of our kerosene lamps, trimmed the wicks, and filled their dimpled glass bases with fuel. A double-acting Meyers pump drew water from our well so that we had pressurized running water, but the pump demanded that each day John must duck into a cave-like well house. For more than twenty minutes, he pushed a lever away from his chest and pulled it back until the pressure gauge read forty pounds. When guests came for the weekend and offered to lend a hand, we sent them to pump water. They never left a faucet running.

Because my engineer father supervised the construction of power plants for Detroit Edison, family discussions about electricity flowed through my childhood. He talked during supper about the re-enforced steel they had laid or how many yards of cement they had poured to build the cooling water towers required for a nuclear power plant. He scattered words such as "turbines" and "generators" through our conversations like sprinkling salt and pepper. On brutal August days, he reported how his company had avoided a brownout by purchasing electricity from hydroelectric plants in Quebec. I envisioned the power humming through hundreds of miles of thick cables and transformers. Because my father helped to create electricity, he respected the effort required to bring it into our home. If my brother or I left a light on after exiting a room, we had to pay him a nickel.

One time while I perused an electronics catalog that featured different make-it yourself kits, he pointed at a radio.

"I made something like that when I was a kid. It worked pretty well." He slipped on his reading glasses and studied the description. Our faces matched: ruddy skin, blonde hair, and glasses. Often our hands worked together as we built dollhouse furniture or sanded a model ship.

"Kids can make radios?" I asked. "Could I make one?"

A few months later, a large, brightly wrapped box waited for me under the Christmas tree, beside the obvious stack of books. I eased off the paper, lifted the lid and stared at the bags of wire, tiny glass cylinders, pieces of metal and a little bag holding an odd honeycombed disk of plastic, a solar cell. "Electrical Experiment Kit," proclaimed a booklet, "for ages twelve and up".

"Start with the first project." My father's thick fingers pointed as he explained the various parts. "Work your way through it. By the end of the manual, you'll build a radio that can run on the solar cell."

On a May afternoon, I positioned the palm-size cell in my bedroom window and waited for a surge of electricity to power my home-built radio. Nothing happened. I fiddled with the solar cell's wires. Still no crackle. Finally, I plugged a cord into the outlet drawing electricity from the power plants built by my father, and music erupted from the speakers.

When John and I moved into our home, we refused to spend thousands of dollars so that we could run electrical lines and connect with the local power company. Some friends and family looked askance at our books on wind generators and solar panels while we criticized nuclear power, including the plant my father's company had built. But now they only asked, when would our home-grown electricity flow through the house? I repeated the same question because a mile west, up in my in-laws' barn sat a large wooden crate filled with the parts for a restored Jacob's wind generator. Dust covered another crate holding the blades that would form the propeller. Once, the turbine had gyrated on a Dakota homestead. By spinning a coil between the poles of a magnet, the generator had sliced the lines of force near the poles, and electricity had pulsed into a remote farm house. Lights had glowed.

The morning after that particularly hot night, John and I sat on our front porch eating breakfast, escaping the heat of the cook stove.

"I've been thinking," John said. "People on an island in Maine are using photovoltaic panels, so why not in Michigan?"

"But we already bought the wind generator."

"We still need to buy a bank of batteries, and a large inverter, and we can't afford either of them this year," John said. "But we could buy one PV panel, set it on the roof, and hook it to a couple of car batteries. That would give us a little juice."

After that year's harvest, John opened a long, narrow box, and we studied the photovoltaic panel. Steel framed the black Plexiglas that trapped circles outlined in yellow crayon, a mass of fish eggs floating in murky pond water. How could this contraption spin the sun's gold into electricity and squeeze it through wires? What if it proved as useless as that tiny solar cell I had held years ago?

"Have to build a wooden rack for it," John said. "I'll need to adjust the angle of the panel as the seasons change so that we'll have maximum exposure to the sun's rays."

"But how does it work?"

John handed me a book. Semiconductors would shuttle the sunlight between two layers of silicon. The rays would snatch an electron from an atom with an extra charge, and slip the electron through the second layer, into a waiting gap, the extended palm of another atom. Electrons would slide back and forth, weaving sunlight into an electrical current.

Later that afternoon, John stood on the house roof, securing the wooden rack and snaking black wires through the ceiling of the porch. That evening, he slid back the calico curtains hiding the space beneath the kitchen counter. More wires ran through the wall to two car batteries hooked to a brown metal box with dials.

"That's the inverter." John pointed to a bread loaf-shaped box. "I bought it from Army surplus. Pretty heavy, so don't try to lift it. When you want electricity, flip this switch and you can plug into this outlet. I'll run an extension cord upstairs and eventually, we'll wire the house."

He flipped the switch; the box hummed. "When you are finished using the blender or whatever, turn off the inverter and unplug the appliance."

"Why?"

"Because it takes electricity to run the inverter, and we can't afford to lose any power by leaving it on. When some appliances are plugged in, they draw a phantom load. You have to unplug everything in order to avoid that loss."

John switched on a floor lamp, and pulled it over to the table. Beneath the counter, the inverter buzzed. He read *The Trees* aloud while I appliquéd pink roses onto a quilt block. Our sons slept in their bunk beds. Coyotes howled from the bog. Suddenly, black dropped over the room. The inverter went silent.

"Guess we need to keep a kerosene lamp lit." John's footsteps tromped across the room. "Never know when the batteries will run out of juice." He set the lamp on the table and struck a match. The wick blazed.

The next spring, I squinted at John's silhouette on the house roof as he finished wiring two more solar panels onto the expanded rack.

"What about the wind generator?" I asked. "Why not set it up?"

"We need to add an insulated room onto the barn for the batteries. We need a good year so that we can buy a larger inverter, that's the missing link."

"A big crop and no big equipment breakdowns, right?" Every year seemed to bring frost or blight, bugs or drought that snatched blueberries from the bushes. And with the adoption of our sons, the farm had to provide for our larger family.

"Yup, need a bumper crop. It'll come one of these days."

On a late-June morning, the beam of John's flashlight illuminated the red line of the thermometer marking twenty-nine degrees. The wind had dwindled and cold had settled in the bog. The tiny green berries shone like rubber beads. I swallowed back tears. Another year of spraying, mowing, and hanging traps; all the while knowing that the harvest would be a smidgen of what we might have reaped.

"How much did we lose?" I asked.

John kicked a frozen clump of grass. "Seventy to seventy-five percent. If we're lucky, the damaged berries will fall off."

"And if they don't?"

"The berries will wither and cling to the stems. When we shake the bushes, some of the dried berries will fall into the lugs with the good berries. The fan on the packing line should blow most of them out, but not the Blue Crop."

"Why not? What's different about that variety?"

"They're too far along, just a few weeks away from harvest. So they will probably turn blue, and some will be real chewy."

"Meaning that we will have to sort more carefully."

"Yup, it will take more time."

"And time is money."

A translucent fiberglass skylight capped the steel roof of my in-law's packing shed. Stacks of brown boxes surrounded me like castle walls, insulating me from the side of the metal pole barn. Our young sons played with toy trucks in a nearby corner. The air throbbed as half a dozen motors growled. Some powered conveyor belts. Others spun a fan that blew leaves, twigs, and now withered fruit from a stream of cascading berries that rolled into a machine filled with hundreds of fiberglass rods that twisted off stems. Plop, plop, the berries dropped into a tank of water. The sweetest and heaviest ones fell to the bottom onto another conveyor belt that rose out of the pool, and slid beneath a blower that dried the fruit. The lighter ones were skimmed off and shot down a chute into a barrel, destined to become juice. A covey of women stood by the last belt, wearing aprons and bandanas, picking out withered berries or separating clusters. While John and I sniffed kerosene at home, in this building we thrust three-prong plugs into the grid in order to pack our fruit,.

Outside, thunder crashed. Lightening snapped. Rain drummed on the metal roof and drowned out the clatter. The fluorescent lights flickered. Motors silenced. Only the storm spoke.

"How long will the power be off?" a worked asked. She stood in the doorway. Rain sheeted off the eaves. Her blue scarf gleamed against the dark landscape.

"I don't know." I sank on the table, and stared at the frozen machinery that would require scores of solar panels to provide enough kilowatts to run the packing line.

A week later, the ring of a phone split a Friday afternoon in July. My mother's voice shook.

"Your father's had a heart attack. The doctors are doing all they can. It doesn't look good."

"Should I start driving?" I calculated the hours it would take me to reach Detroit.

"No, wait. I'll call later."

I stumbled through the afternoon, caring for our boys, cooking dinner, waiting for the phone to ring. Finally, some force pulled me onto the porch swing. A sudden breeze rushed through the lilacs and poplars. A hush surrounded me. I knew my father was gone.

Several hours later, my mother called. My father's heart had stopped. The sparks at the nerve endings had faded. Within his brain, the crackle of ideas had ceased. The man who had built power plants lay still as the tiny solar cell he had placed in my hand.

The lights were too bright in the funeral parlor. The mounds of flowers overpowered the perfumes and aftershaves that floated from the scores of visitors. The day's events blurred as the current of visitation and burial mingled.

"Too young," the mourners said, shaking their heads. "He had just retired." Their arms embraced my mother, her gray head pressed against their shoulders.

My sons clung to me, shy in the unstable land of grieving. Only six and eight years old, would they remember their grandfather? Poverty had induced their birth mother to abandon them, now death denied them another relationship. After the funeral, they played with puppets dressed in blue silk and turbans, a gift from relatives.

On the ride home to our farm, I stared at my hands. The pressure of the mourners' fingers lingered as did their words of praise for my father, who had helped provide electricity for thousands of homes. Why hadn't I affirmed his labors?

I escaped to my treadle sewing machine, and picked up the triangles and squares I had cut out before last Friday's phone call. The needle flashed through layers of black, purple and maroon.

My hands guided the fabric just as my mother had taught me as a child. The solid colors gyrated into pinwheels. I sliced more cloth. In a month, I pieced three quilt tops.

In the late fall, I reread my mother's note. *Use it for something special.* I scanned her check.

"Buy the inverter." I handed it to John.

I walked through the bog, blueberry leaves as dark as ox blood. Tears blurred my path. Negative and positive electrons circled around the nucleus of my soul. The daughter, who had criticized her father's nuclear power plants, gratefully accepted an unmerited check that would power her home. The bountiful harvest, the little extra that the land refused to provide had come from the electrical network constructed by my father.

Holding our sons' hands, John and I stood on Pleasant Hill, and watched the red bullet-shaped wind generator turn into the breeze. The propeller-like blades fluttered and picked up speed. They sliced the wind into millions of notes that hummed through the wires running into the battery room. Wonder spun inside me, for the grace of my mother's check, and for John's ability to connect wind and wires to power our home. We ran into the earth-bermed room where tall glass cylinders bubbled as electricity charged the batteries. I pulled a string, and light illuminated the inverter's gauges. With each gust, the black needles in the circles leapt and danced.

SOUP FOR THE SOIL

"For the Lord delights in you,
And to Him your land will be married."
Isaiah 62:4

Clomp. Clomp. Clomp. John's work boots stomped upon the wooden floor of our porch. I looked up from my writing.

"Yes?"

"I forgot to buy molasses. I have to have it for my compost tea. Can you run to the feed mill for me? I need baking yeast, too."

"How much yeast do you want?" I shoved paper and pen to one side of our table and stepped to the gas refrigerator.

"A pound."

"All I have is a pound, minus a little." I held out the red and white bag. Above the brand name, the smiling male baker shook yeast into a bowl half his size.

"Can't you buy more? I have to have it now. And please go to the feed mill for molasses." John strode away. "I'll put a five-gallon bucket in the back of the car."

I picked up my car keys. Out in the barnyard, John hovered

over a large fiberglass tub, fiddling with an electric bubbler that circulated five hundred gallons of dingy pond water. Bits of straw and leaves floated over the surface, and began to dance when John plugged in the bubbler.

"What's in it?" I sniffed.

"Compost. Manure. Your yeast. A few magic ingredients, like seaweed. It still needs molasses to feed the yeast."

"'Double, double, toil and trouble,'" I chanted. "'Fire burn and caldron bubble.'" I opened the car door, and sped away.

Standing at the mill, I listened to the chug of engines grinding corn and mixing feed. Chaff drifted in the sunbeams. One of the resident gray cats ran up, activated the automatic sliding glass door, and trotted inside. A country music song slipped through the opening. At the loading dock, a school of pick-ups, red, blue, and silver, surrounded my green Subaru station wagon. English sparrows pecked at spilled grain. Across the road, the corn stood waist high. A blonde teenage girl trundled out a dolly carrying my bucket of molasses.

"Sorry it's sticky. Want me to put it in your car?" She jumped off the deck, and hoisted the bucket into the car. "Have a good one!" Her ponytail flipped as she turned away.

"Thanks!" I scrutinized her biceps, and wondered how many tons she lifted in a day.

Back at home, John poured a fragrant brown stream of molasses into his tub, paused, eyed the bucket, and added another cup. This was a man who claimed he could only scramble eggs and slap together PBJ sandwiches. As the bubbler churned the brew, a fine mist rose, and the air smelled like the great fermenting vats of rum I had observed years ago in Puerto Rico.

"How do you know what to do?"

"I read about compost tea in my organic farming magazine. And I talked to my fertilizer consultant out in Arizona."

John should have added *for hours* to the last clause. Whenever I found my normally reticent husband chattering on the phone, I knew the conversation focused on some new organic fertilizer or technique he had read about. Soon semi trucks would rumble up our half-mile driveway hauling loads of steaming compost, and the UPS driver would unload bags of humates or buckets of concentrated sea water. Jugs of neem oil distilled from trees in India lined the walls of John's spray shed. A fifty-five gallon drum of odiferous fish emulsion sat outside it. He continuously experimented, trying to find the most efficient pest controls and the best organic fertilizers.

"Why don't you take notes?" I had once suggested. "You could write an article for your organic farming magazine. You could tell others what worked, and describe your mistakes so they wouldn't repeat them."

"Nah. One writer in the family's enough."

On our evening walks, John was a doctor making his rounds. He noted the color of blueberry branches and leaves. He checked the twigs, scanning them for signs of botrytis, a mold that attacks and kills branches. He frowned at wilted shoots, and scowled at Japanese beetles chomping on leaves. While I listened to the call of a barred owl, John studied the dirt. His beloved. The other woman in my life.

"I've got to get some water on these bushes. The sun's baking the soil. But I think those trace minerals are helping. Look at all the new growth."

The next day, I stepped back from the stinking vat. "How long's this supposed to work? Smells like you *did* add eye of newt and toe of bat!"

"Supposed to work five days!" John's right arm was submerged to his elbow as he held one end of a hose near the bottom of the vat. With his left hand he gripped the other end of the hose on the surface of the tea. A gas engine roared. The brew churned and roiled, as the hoses sucked and spewed the tea, mixing the mess.

"Going anaerobic on me!" John yelled. "Have to spray it out!"

"Now? It's supper time."

"Gotta put out a tank first!" John draped a hose end over the tub. Tea streamed over the surface and splattered him. He flipped the engine's switch and dragged his sleeve across his face.

"Go ahead and eat. Save me a plate. I'll be in after this tank. I'll still have three more loads to go after this one. Going be a late night."

John loved a good meal, but that night he fed the land. In the gloaming, I sat on the porch swing and read Annie Dillard's prose.

Another year, another summer season. Gone were the tanks of manure tea and aquarium bubblers. Like any chef, John had perfected his recipe and techniques for brewing the perfect compost tea. In the bay of the barn, a large plastic container encaged by a metal grid work sat on a wooden pallet. John had sliced the top off of the tank and now he leaned into it, arranging pipes that he had welded to a stainless steel bowl. The gizmo looked like Tom Terrific, a cartoon character of my childhood. Sun glinted on a new bubbler, a large pump intended for aerating ponds. When I asked how much it cost, John sent me to a weekend writing conference.

"How much oatmeal you got?" The plastic muffled his voice.

"About five pounds." *Not this again*, I inwardly moaned. Six pounds of brewer's yeast lingered in my chest freezer because this summer's tea recipe did not require it.

"Can I have it? Please? And next time you go to the coop, buy me fifty pounds."

"Do you know how big a fifty pound bag of oatmeal is?"

"Make it twenty-five." John jumped off the pallet.

"Quick or regular?" I quipped.

"Quick. Here." He handed me a cardboard box containing a transparent bag filled with a crumbly black substance.

"What is it?" I sniffed, but could not place the scent. "Compost?"

"Nope. Alaska humus."

"Didn't you already try this stuff, years ago?"

"Yeah. But this time, I'm making tea with it. Please mix this with some oatmeal, and set the whole thing in a warm spot."

"It's July. It's warm everywhere. Can't it stay out here?"

"It has to be at a constant temperature. We're cultivating good fungi, like when you make yogurt."

"Will it smell?"

"Shouldn't.

I stuck the box in a corner near our wood-burning cook stove, the same place where I cultured French goat cheese. Now, I grew fungi.

A few days later, John turned back the box's flaps. "Mold's ready."

I peeked and smelled my garden after a spring rain. Fine white threads laced through the humus and oatmeal like a Shetland shawl.

"Great stuff." John beamed. "Wait and see, bet the blueberries grow three feet." He strode out with his treasure chest under his arm, and paused. "How cool is it going to be tonight?"

"Hmm, seventy now, I think tonight will be in the fifties."

"That's why I have my tank on a pallet. I can forklift it into the barn and keep it warm."

The next morning, while I was writing, John rushed in. "You *have* to come see."

I put down my pen and followed him to the barnyard.

"Look!" John waves his arm. "Just the way tea is supposed to be; even smells right."

The motor of the aerator hummed. Atop the bubbling brew, a foot of foam quivered, the color of chocolate mousse. Like a simmering volcano, the foam expanded, and a large dollop tumbled onto the cement barn floor. The odor of mushrooms surrounded the tub. Another dollop plopped onto the floor.

"Amazing. And you think this stuff will work magic?"

"Yup. It will feed good fungus to the soil and plants. The good guys will boost the plant's immune system and beat out the bad fungus…should stop the gray mold. Plus healthier soil grows healthy plants that will make nutrient dense blueberries."

"Did you write down this particular recipe?"

"Nope. Did you mark down the last time I sprayed? I keep forgetting."

"Yes. I've been keeping track in my weather journal."

"Thanks. I'll start spraying after lunch. Going to rain tonight, right? Need to get it on the plants before then."

"Supposed to. Think you could spray some on my tomatoes, please? Might help ward off blight."

"Yup."

All afternoon John sprayed his tea upon the blueberry bushes and soil. After sunset, thunder rolled in, and John stood on the porch, gloating. In farming, timing is everything, and this time, the farmer and the weather danced

"What's the weather suppose to be like next Friday?" John asked. "Warm enough for brewing tea?

It appeared that soup for the soil would be a regular item on our summer's menu.

Saint George and the Dragon

"The Lord will continually guide you,
And satisfy your desire in scorched places"
Isaiah 58: 11

All fall a dragon flew over our farm, and his breath seared the land, robbing moisture from the humus. Under normal climatic condition, when the soil is saturated, it attracts clouds. But without magnetic moisture sandwiched between the clay and sand particles, the clouds rising off of Lake Michigan scooted inland. The drought that began in the fall stalked the land through December. The dragon's glassy stare froze the land, and ice crystals crusted the hay fields. Our boots crunched against the glittered shards as we scanned the dirt, hoping the wildflower seeds we had planted in October would survive the subzero nights.

While standing in line at the library, I listen to a hatless and mittenless woman and the librarian laud the winter sunshine, the clear roads, and clean cars not smeared by salt. I wanted to tell the two women that the land *needs* snow, and plants appreciate the insulation. Across the street, youths in shorts and T-shirts shot baskets on New Year's Eve. Don't they miss sledding or skiing? I wondered as I plunked down my books. Come April, will they know the thrill of leaving long underwear slumped on the bedroom floor while they search behind the pile of boots for their dusty sneakers? Like the fruits and vegetables flown around the globe and deposited in the produce aisle, our lives defied the dimly lit days of winter. We jogged through the seasonal hush and ignored the pleasures of sunlight glinting on ice-covered lakes, etched by the blades of our ice skates.

A snowless winter folded into a dry spring. Only wispy clouds licked the sky and dissipated when they moved over the lakeshore. A haze of dust enveloped our neighbor's tractor as he disked his orchards.

"It's April," farmers commented when they bumped into each other at the hardware, their lightweight jackets unzipped. "Where's the rain?" These were the months when rain should pelt the earth, fill the ditches, and enlarge the irrigation ponds. Instead mud cracks split the ground where puddles normally formed ruts. Turkey and deer stamped tracks into the oozy bottoms of the blueberry ditches, and the muskrats escaped into our pond. In a spasm of unseasonable heat, daffodils blossomed and withered. The sprinklers in my kitchen garden whirred, soaking the potatoes, onions, and the pea seedlings. Lilacs erupted into purple fountains, but the dry air stifled their scent.

"This is ridiculous," I muttered as I positioned a soaker hose in a flowerbed. Where were the spring showers of my childhood?

Those gray afternoons when rain streaked the school windows as our hands taped up bright construction paper umbrellas. Rows of red, black and white rubber boots waited in the cloakroom for the walk home through puddles.

The dragon hovered; his heat poured over us. On the eighth of May, a month earlier than normal, John rumbled through the alfalfa, the haybine's teeth chomping. Our first cutting fell in thin swaths that spiraled from the center of the field like limp twine. Swallows darted behind John, snatching the insects as they rose from the plants. John's straw hat shaded his face; his blue short-sleeved shirt fluttered in the breeze.

Three days later, we stacked only a hundred bales. "Not good," John said. "Normally that field should yield four hundred or more bales. It's just too dry. We might get a second cutting, but I doubt if there'll be a third."

We sat on a bale still warm from the day's heat and stared out the barn door towards the sunset. I handed John a cup of lemonade. We had endured droughts before, but never had the dragon struck so early, so deeply; already, John had set his lips into a thin line.

In June, the dragon laughed, and hot winds sucked the remaining moisture from the soil, leaves and plant stems. Sand sifted across the surface of my garden as if the carrots grew on a desert dune. Quartz and feldspar crystals tumbled between the plants as I weeded and mulched them. Grit coated my lips. The wind dug hollows around the broccoli stems. The lack of rain sliced farmers' hearts; the winds drove salt into the wounds.

"Isn't this wonderful?" two women dressed in tank tops, shorts, and sandals said as they leaned against their carts, talking in the grocery store. "Great beach weather. And so early."

The dog days of July had struck in June, and I felt like snarling at the duo. But if I hadn't married a farmer with his brown forearms and white biceps, come Saturday, I would probably have spread a towel on the beach. As a child, playing with my cousins on their farm, I had overheard my aunt and uncle discuss frosts and dry spells, but I had not understood the impact of the elements on their grape harvest. My cousins and I had simply pushed aside the screen door, and dashed through the vineyards.

"Here." John looped a hose onto a hook positioned near the tractor seat. The hose connected to a spray rig that was attached to the tractor's power-take-off shaft. "Drive in second or third low, and aim the nozzle at the base of each blueberry bush. Count to thirty and move on. That should soak the ground." He dragged his sleeve across his forehead. We expected to water plants in July, but not in June.

I lumbered down the farm lane on the Massey Ferguson tractor, my feet dangling a few inches from the pedals. Dust billowed around me, burning my nostrils. The spray rig bounced behind the tractor; the long red tube held four hundred gallons of water, and had a large fan attached to the rear end, a metallic tail. A dozen or more small nozzles were strung along the back rim near the fan. Normally, John filled the tank with compost tea or foliar fertilizers; the jets spewed out the solution, the fan whirred, and a spray covered the bushes. He repeated the process every few weeks until the episodes blurred; our neighbors performed the same labor. Many chose to spray at night after the winds subsided, the high whine of their spray rigs rippling across acres of apples and peaches. Like recognizing the opening notes of a fiddle tune, John could discern the voice of each spray rig and declare which neighbor rolled through his orchard.

I squirted and drove, squirted and drove. Different rhythms punctuate farming: the ping of maple sap into a metal bucket, the chug of a baler scooping up, and spitting out bales, the crunch of a goat's teeth on corn. The time signature varies with the seasons; the mode influences the mood. Harvest accelerates the pace into dozens of sixteenth notes. But sometimes the beat dissolves in the struggle to survive. As I wound between the rows I wondered how Agnes Wadsworth, the woman who had originally planted these bushes, had coped with the dragon of drought. Had she played her piano to drive away the gloom? Or stared at the irises in her garden before appliquéing the drooping flowers in shades of blue, purple, and gold onto a quilt that I now cherish?

In 1937, despite the pall of the economy and hot, dry summers, Dwight and Agnes Wadsworth cleared a few acres of brush from their peat bog, leaving one white pine for shade. On his steel-tired tractor, Dwight puttered back and forth, the disk slicing the peat, releasing that peculiar spicy smell; a scent of ancient leaf mold and thatched grass mingled with a trace of cloves. He and Agnes hammered in scores of short stakes and tied string to the markers, and dreamt of cultivating high bush blueberries, a crop grown mainly on the East Coast. Into the soil they patted rooted blueberry cuttings, single stalks about eight inches high with a few tiny twigs and leaves. They chose two varieties: Rubles whose firm berries would ooze flavor into muffins and pies, and Jerseys whose powdery blue skin would shelter sun-spun sugar. The two pioneers rubbed the dirt from their hands, leaned against their wagon, and posed for a photo that their great-nephew had shown us. Soon, John's grandfather followed their leading. Dwight and Agnes had envisioned the blueberry plantation that I now watered.

In mid-June, our friend, Brad and I stitched a dragon. His auburn curls fluffed about his sweaty face as he lay on his side, and his freckled fingers stretched green fabric across a chicken wire frame that he had attached to a small wheelbarrow. Once the dragon had defended Brad's master of fine arts thesis, and had transformed him into a puppeteer on a children's television show. Now his beast's rainbow-colored body wallowed on the floor of my barn, waiting for tomorrow's production. As my fingers pulled a needle, the irony settled into my senses. At last year's party, we had decided that for the next solstice we would dramatize the story of Saint George the Dragon Slayer. Was our decision prophetic or prompted by providence?

A week later on the afternoon of the solstice, Brad lugged trunks of costumes and props into our barn. The cast of friends collected their garb. Carlos slipped into the butterfly wings we had created. Matt pinned orange, scarlet and gold leaves onto his overalls and plastered a rainbow cap over his black hair.

Darrell donned a leather vest, and slapped on a World War I helmet. "Hides my bald spot," he said.

"*I'm* to be queen," his wife, Connie said, as she placed a silver crown on her head. Tall and blonde, her curls frizzed over a black velvet cape.

"Well, we get enough of management every week," Kay said. "We're being peasants." Kay squashed a mop cap over her black hair, and tied the laces of a gray cloak that hid most of her short frame. Her husband, Dan pulled on a yellow and blue smock.

"And I shall be king." Louie strutted across the stage, twirling his maroon cape. Six feet up, his gold crown sparkled.

"All right," Deborah said. "Let's practice."

By late afternoon, two-dozen cars parked along the fence surrounding my kitchen garden. The adults stood in the shade and sipped punch, discussing burnt lawns and withering gardens. Finally, the drought had scratched everyone's lives. Older children tossed a Frisbee in the field below the barn while others played on a hay wagon.

"John, blow on your tuba," Deborah said. "That'll bring in the kids."

John lifted his silver tuba, and blasted out a cascading crescendo. Feet pounded up the hill and sounded on the wooden steps leading through the barn. Children shimmered in the heat waves. Some of the girls wore nineteenth century calico dresses over bloomers, while suspenders held up some of the boy's jeans. Others ran in t-shirts and shorts. Round and slim, gangly or graceful, small and tall, they pelted up the hill.

"What was *that*?" a gaggle of boys asked.

"The dragon sneezed." Brad's gray eyes teased. Tiny navy stars swirled over his billowing Victorian shirt.

"What dragon?"

"Come one! Come all! Come into this hall!" Deborah banged a bodhran. Her olive-green skirt fanned across the grass.

Parents clustered with their children on the floor or wooden chairs. Overhead, the metal roof creaked and expanded beneath the sun's glare. A breeze tickled the pines to the east of the barn. Grinning behind his beard, Dave played *When the Saints Come Marching In* on his accordion. John, wearing a white smock and gold halo, strode with Darrell down the center aisle of the barn to a small stage.

"Hey, it's *my* saint's day! June 24th, the feast of Saint John." John motioned to cut the music. "And I *am* Saint John. Who are you?"

"St. George. Everyone forgot about my feast." Darrell lifted his broadsword. "I heard there was a dragon lurking about." A roar rose through the floorboards from the second level of the barn where Brad hid.

"A dragon!" the thespians screamed.

"What are we going to do?" Queen Connie asked.

"We could feed him our livestock," King Louie said.

Matt and Carlos marched down the center aisle, hugging two baby goats. "We offer these." They descended the stairs leading to the second story, into the dragon's lair.

"More!" the dragon shouted. "I want the princess!"

"Good gentlemen and ladies," St. George said. "Spare the damsel. I will slay the dragon if you will give me her hand in marriage."

"Yes!" King Louie shouted.

"Follow me!" St. George called.

114

Everyone charged out the double doors, and onto the hill where the Chinese dragon snapped its jaws. White teeth spiked the giant mouth, softball eyes glared above red nostrils. A dozen children's feet inched down the hillside; their hands gripped tubes that supported the purple and orange netting forming the dragon's long body. St. George pranced about the beast's head, circled his sword and struck. The dragon gasped, screamed, and collapsed. The crowd cheered. We flowed back into the barn towards tables smothered with casseroles and salads. After the feast, we pulled out accordions and fiddles, and lit into reels that drove the dancers' feet.

For a few hours, the agony of the soil receded from our minds. We dwelled in the mystery of the myth, the triumph of humanity. If only we could simply call forth a saint who would slay the fiery beast that fried our fields. But the leaves on our bushes still sagged, and tomorrow we would face the foe once again. Where are you Saint George, whose name means man from the earth?

By mid-July withered berries hung like clusters of raisins. Leaves turned yellow. Young canes died. Brown streaked the fields as if a painter had shaken his brush. Not only were we losing this year's crop, but also next year's. Usually after harvest, the bushes formed buds that would bloom the following spring. Now, they hunkered in survival mode unable to draw the strength to create buds. The effects of the drought would haunt next year.

One afternoon, John clattered into the bog hauling a Traveler, a portable irrigation system that belonged to our neighbor, Rob. A few hours later, he dragged in another offering from a friend,

Eddie's trailer of six-inch irrigation pipe. That evening, Eddie helped John connect a half-mile conduit to a portable irrigation pump that they positioned at a far back pond. John stumbled home as the last glimmer in the west faded into a smear of lavender. Dust coated his clothes.

"We'll turn the Traveler on tomorrow," he said. Our shoulders brushed as we rocked on the porch swing. My bare feet rested on his. "Thank God for friends," he said. "We'll make it through this."

The next morning, I heard the faint chugging of an engine and slipped down to the bog. Yesterday, John had hooked a tractor to the Traveler's long hose and unrolled it from a giant wheel. Now, a tractor parked by the back pond powered an irrigation pump that pushed water through the half-mile of irrigation pipes, into the hose, and out the jet that blasted a spray across the bushes. As the water gushed through the hose, it also powered a small turbine connected to the giant wheel, and the turbine generated power that retracted the hose. Like a woodpecker's tongue, the coiling hose pulled the sprinkler back down the row as the hose wound onto the wheel.

Droplets dimpled the black silt. Robins and brown thrashers flitted in and out of the shower created by the huge sprinkler. John and his berry bushes were not the only ones weary for water. Near the edge of the bog, the bottom of a swale shimmered like coal. Jewelweed hung over the banks, and the hoof prints of deer freckled the muck where the animals had come to drink and found only mud. A great blue heron flew overhead, another refugee displaced by empty blueberry ditches.

A decade ago, I had hopped between puddles, searching for a dry spot where I could stand and pick blueberries. Rainy days had interrupted the harvest. John had kept a bulldozer parked at the end of the rows, so that when the blueberry shaker mired in the soggy peat, he could pull it out of the ruts. And now we begged for moisture. Each morning for a week, John unlocked the pipes, moved them to where bushes were dying, and fitted the great straws back together. A teasing haze smudged the sky in the late afternoons, but the only rumble came from the tractor's engine.

We stood by our pew on an August Sunday morning as the minister prayed. He pleaded for peace and for healing for those suffering from diseases. He prayed for rain, for relief from the drought for farmers. I bit my lower lip, tears prickled my eyelids, but my will could not hold them back. Someone had finally discerned the anguish of the few, the less than one percent of the population, who work the land. My hand grabbed John's. I thought of the fields we had driven past that morning, of yellow cornstalks with leaves curled so tightly they resemble tops of pineapples. We grieved as the land clutched at our lives.

That evening, John dragged out his piano accordion and soared into a rake of reels. He filled himself with the music that had endured blights and famines, and a voyage to a new world. Even the names of the tunes spoke of the land: *The Wind that Shakes the Barley*, *The Smell of the Bog*, and *The New Mown Meadow*. Finally, he squeezed the bellows in, latched them, and stared out at our dwindling pond.

"I've never seen it so dry. I heard yesterday that a couple of irrigation ponds went dry on blueberry farms north of Holland. Not much more a farmer can do when he can't pump water."

"Should we give up?" I asked.

"It's crossed my mind." John set down his accordion and sprawled in his chair.

"We could go back to school. You could try a class at the seminary."

"And be a preacher like my grandfather?" John said.

"Why not? You love reading theology."

"But my grandfather gave up preaching and bought the farm. And I hate writing papers."

"Well, should I look for a part time teaching job?" I gazed through a mirage at a world that might offer health insurance, air conditioned offices, and colleagues who read books. Yet wiser friends had pointed out that adjunct professors were like migrant teachers who wander between campuses, teaching one course here and another there, not earning much money.

"No, you're worth more to me here, driving tractors, filling in the gaps. Let's face it. We wouldn't be happy doing anything else."

John was right. For too many years, our lives had been carved by the tilt of the earth, and the angle of the sun. The farm was our identity. When we picked up the phone we answered, "Pleasant Hill", the name of the farm and not with our own names.

I fled to my basket of fabric and pulled out color. Blue, dark green, red and yellow, I sliced them into squares and triangles. At least my quilts provided added cash during a slim season. Just as Agnes Wadsworth stitched lavender irises during the Depression,

I sewed the shapes into the pattern called the anvil. The colors throbbed against a black background. I smoothed the square and prayed that a cumulus cloud would rise to the west. That thousands of convection cells would expand and lengthen into a black ridge and send streaks of lightning through our sky.

On an August morning, a hurricane struck the Gulf Coast, hundreds of miles south of Michigan. Mare's tail clouds rippled across the southwestern sky as the moisture from the Gulf crept northward. The black needle on the barometer fell rapidly during the afternoon as the restless air expanded in heat. The goats skittered away from us. The bees crawled on the outside of their hives, and chased anyone who walked near them.

Thunder muttered out on Lake Michigan, and the wind flipped the leaves on the maples, turning them into silver bangles. Clouds bruised the west, smothering the sun. I ran and closed the goat barn doors that had stood open so long, that cobwebs draped the gaps between the hinges and barn siding. Gusts of wind bent the tops of the sassafras trees, and tossed thin twigs that clattered onto the wood shed's tin roof. A few fat raindrops pocked the soil and lifted the scent of dust. A vortex swirled above me as cold and warm air clashed. Gray clouds tangled with black. Where were John and the boys? I ran inside our house, and prayed that they were safe.

The dragon screamed. The earth cried out. St. George wielded his sword. Lightning veined the sky. Curtains of rain dragged over the fields. Thunder vibrated the windowpanes. The claws of the dragon ripped branches; limbs crashed. Lightning blasted a nearby tree. Electricity snapped from the outlets. The dragon beat his wings and charged. The trees moaned.

St. George pierced the dragon's belly. Rain surged and pummeled the earth. Hail chattered against the skylight. Water sluiced down the windows. Wind drove the rain horizontally under the sashes, and flashes of lightning illuminated waterfalls cascading onto the floor. I grabbed a basket of dirty laundry, and dumped it on the puddles. All the hoarded precipitation descended; wave upon wave struck the soil as the heavenly battle engulfed us.

Finally, the trees twisted as a north wind invaded, driving the storm eastward. The rain drifted into a veil, and wrapped itself about the land. Standing on the porch, I listened to the thunder receding and inhaled the richness of soaked soil. The tree frogs sang. Brown froth tumbled down the driveway through a rain-dug gorge, and filled a large puddle in the middle of my flower garden where our ducks paddled.

John dashed onto the porch. "We were caught in the barn. The wind drove the rain through every knothole and crack. The boys are still there, playing basketball."

"Did you check the rain gauge?"

"Over three inches. I figured those were seventy-mile-an-hour winds. Probably knocked several hundred pounds of berries on the ground." John shook his head. "It took a hurricane down south to bring rain to the north."

"But it *rained*." I thanked God for every drop, for giving back the harvest. I didn't want to tally the losses, not yet. I wanted to inhale the moist air and feel it deep in my lungs. Raindrops dripped off the clematis leaves that clung to the screens and cloaked the porch. The soaked phlox flowers bowed, spattered with dirt. The rooster crowed and reclaimed the day.

After the rain ceased, the boys rode off on their bikes while John and I walked through the farm, surveying the fallen trees; the deep ruts cut into the farm roads, and flattened rye fields. We met our neighbor, Rob, who rented John's parents' peach orchard. Dozens of fruit trees were bent over with half of their roots ripped from the soil, limbs heavy with ripening fruit snapped off, and leaves littered the earth.

"Think they'll live?" I asked.

John and Rob stared at the tangled roots.

"Hopefully," John said.

"We'll stake them. Some will make it," Rob said. "Could be worse. Up on his hill, Gary lost three hundred trees."

I glanced at the guys as they leaned against Rob's pick-up. Their conversation shifted from the damage that erased years of labor to how to revive their fields. They were already claiming the future. I walked home.

Leaves drifted over the surface of our pond. Webs of twigs and grass bobbed near shore. For now the dragon had flown, but the struggle never ends. A truce held tonight. A cardinal sang, and green tinted the roots of the grass. I began to pick up sticks, clearing the land.

SCATTERED JEWELS

One spring, while thumbing through seed catalogs, I gazed at the photographs of meadows dotted with daisies, sprinkled with scarlet poppies, and crowned with golden coreopsis. I determined to create such a sight, and pestered John until he disked up an eighth of an acre for me.

Back and forth I trudged, leveling the ground with a rake, and tossing seeds. A phoebe called from the nearby peach tree as he watched me. Off to the west, gray clouds hung low over Lake Michigan, and I quickened my step. A spring shower would be the perfect blessing to help the seeds swell and germinate. Despite my efforts, only a few larkspurs towered pink and blue above the quack grass that choked most of the baby plants. Most likely, mice, voles and starlings had eaten the seeds.

"If you wanted to beat out the weeds, you should have cover-cropped the field with rye and then buckwheat, before planting the flowers," John said.

"Why didn't you tell me that last fall?"

"You didn't ask."

I tucked my flowery vision into a corner of my mind, and plotted to try again some other time. When Carlos' bee business expanded to 60 hives, many of our dinner discussions focused on the problem of "nectar valleys," those times in the growing season when bees have trouble finding an adequate source of nectar. Spring flowers and blooming orchards allowed the bees to fill their supers swiftly in May, but come late June and early July, the nectar supply dropped.

"We need more flowers," John said, a rare statement from a man who teases me about encircling my vegetable garden with old roses.

"How many flowers?" I asked.

"Acres and acres of flowers," John answered.

My dream of wild flower fields shimmered once again.

Ever the scientist, John called wild flower seed companies and requested information on which of those seeds were similar in size to clover seed. He chatted with the experts and explained that he wanted to plant a bed of clover beneath the flowers, so all the seeds must roll through his seed drill. Plus he wanted flowers suited for our climate and soil. Soon, the UPS truck rumbled up our lane and dropped off sacks of daisy, larkspur, bachelor buttons, and red poppy seeds.

In October when the blueberry leaves turned the bog maroon, John planted thirty acres with wildflower and clover seeds. On walks, I taught him how to identify the different seedlings. Lake effect snow finally insulated and protected the baby plants until the Chinooks of spring blew across our farm.

The orange wallflowers first sprinkled the patchwork of green leaves. Soon daisies sparkled among the blue bachelor buttons, and red poppies shimmered here and there until the fields blazed. Bob-o-links took a liking to the sight and nested among the flowers; their bubbling call mingled with the hum of bees. Friends and strangers came to view the spectacle while Carlos stacked supers of honey.

Although Carlos no longer keeps bees, the tradition of sowing fields of wildflowers flourishes. Friends photograph brides and grooms or grandchildren standing midst the poppies; visitors gape at the waves of color. Yet, what thrills me most are the rogue flowers planted by birds or jostled out of the seed drill as it bumped from one field to another section of the farm. A single red poppy lights a blueberry row. The sapphire of a bachelor button sparkles at the edge of the asparagus patch.

They remind me of one midsummer party when my friend Deborah told the children that the queen of the fairies had broken her necklace in our cherry orchard. Earlier that morning Deborah had flung fistfuls of red, green, yellow, and blue plastic beads throughout the orchard. The children crept between the trees collecting plastic gems that they strung into necklaces. For years after that party, my sons continued to stumble upon plastic jewels when they played in that location.

Like the queen of fairies' lost treasure, rubies, sapphires, and opals now glitter in far corners of our farm. I not only have fields filled with flowers, but hidden jewels waiting to be discovered.

WOOD

"Each will be like a refuge from the wind,
Like a refuge from the storm."
Psalm 32: 2

Snowflakes erased the taillights of John's truck and filled the tire tracks. The pines surrounding our home bellowed. The wind blasted snow into the grooves between tree bark. Ice crystals frosted the storm windows and blanketed the skylights. Our timber-framed house creaked as the beams shuddered. I stood alone, and watched the late afternoon February landscape fold into gray and white.

"Should I stay?" John had asked before picking up his suitcase and departing for a week in Honduras. "I don't like leaving you in this. Especially when it will be hard to call."

"Somebody's got to stay with the goats. And you need time with your siblings. The storm's only supposed to last a day or two. And you've left plenty of wood."

Many miles to the west, polar air raced across Lake Michigan unhindered by the surface tension created by trees or buildings.

Like lips stained with blackberry juice, the clouds sucked up heat and moisture from the upper layer of water, yet deep within the lungs of the clouds, the air remained frigid. The cumulus clouds expanded until they rammed into the Michigan lakeshore and spewed snow.

By morning, three-foot drifts blocked the path to the goat shed. Scottish blood simmers in my veins; I layered two pair of socks, long underwear, and sank my feet into felt pack boots. My cranberry red mittens flashed as I thrust a snow shovel into the packed strata of a drift. White above, white below, white swallowed the big barn, the orchard on the hill, and the web of blueberry bushes in the bog. Spencer sat in an upper window of the goat barn, watching me tunnel with my snow shovel. I inhaled the scent of wet wool and denim as my body's heat melted the flakes striking my jacket. The weatherman's voice circled in my head: "Unprotected skin will freeze when exposed for longer than thirty minutes." How long had I been shoveling? The goats bawled, pleading to be fed. And the pregnant does could deliver at any time. Something scarlet flopped and fluttered at the base of pine. I squinted through the white veil at a cardinal. Did the cold claim his life? After clearing the path, I refilled the wood box, and hoped that the four-high foot stack would last the week.

Twenty-five years earlier on a late November afternoon, I had returned home from running errands and stood by the woodshed. Raw air scraped my nostrils like cockleburs, as I surveyed the cord mound of logs, and nudged a few woodchips with the toe of my work boot. Only a few split logs littered the trampled snow. The hydraulic log splitter and tractor had vanished. Where *was* John?

I found no note on the counter when I set down my parcels. While stoking the wood stove, my ears strained for the chug of a returning tractor. The phone rang, and John's father's voice filled my ear.

"We're up in Grand Rapids at Butterworth Hospital. John cut off a finger. They're going to operate."

Gale force winds shook me. Frost rose in my veins. "I'm coming," I said, and hung up. My hands trembled as I called my friend, Lisa.

"John's in GR. He cut off a finger. I don't think I can drive...." Cold swallowed me, numbing my lips.

"I'll be there in a few minutes."

Lisa understood shock and sudden loss. Four years earlier, one of her brothers had accepted a dare and had jumped into an industrial trash compactor. An electronic eye sparked a switch, and Kris lost the lower section of his legs. Three weeks after her brother's accident, Lisa's newborn daughter had lived less than two hours.

Dampen the stove. Draw the shades, my mind ordered. In the flame of a kerosene lamp, my hands swaddled the room, snuffing out the remaining twilight. Piano, sofa, rocking chair mutated into black boulders. The headlights of Lisa's car flickered around a curve in the driveway; craggy sassafras branches slashed the beams. I blew out the lamp, and dashed from the dark.

"Thanks for coming." I tugged on the stiff seatbelt.

"Here." Lisa snapped the metal lock and squeezed my hand. "Man, you're cold."

I nodded and slumped in my seat.

"Don't worry. Butterworth's a good hospital." A stocking cap covered her short black hair. A few inches above five feet, Lisa and I could see eye to eye. She shifted into third gear and continued talking. Her voice lapped across my mind, small waves smoothing a sandy shore. I burrowed into my coat and stuffed my hands beneath my armpits. Back and forth her words rolled. Snowflakes splattered against the windshield.

We flashed by red taillights and the reflectors marking the exits. The shaggy voices of farmers telling about their equipment accidents tumbled in my brain. One friend had a scar running the length of his forearm, a reminder of the afternoon his corn picker had snatched his arm. Another man had almost lost his leg when the power-take-off shaft caught his pants and wrapped the fabric around its shaft.

"Farming is one of the ten most dangerous occupations," John often stated before telling about the time his caterpillar had almost rolled over him while he had rumbled along a ditch bank. The ground had given way underneath, the machine began to flip, and John had jumped to level land. But this afternoon, he had not jerked free in time to clear the splitter's blade.

"College Avenue, right?" Lisa asked.

"Yes, there should be signs."

We trolled College, squinting through the snow. People trudged by dark shop windows. Suddenly, snowflakes wrestled in the red glow spelling, *EMERGENCY.*

"I'll park. Go on in."

Glass doors slid open. Snow followed me into the warmth. Fluorescent lights hummed. A curved desk buttressed the entrance. In her turquoise scrub, the gatekeeper demanded details.

"Patient's name?"

"John Van Voorhees."

"Your name? Relationship?"

"Joan Donaldson, wife."

She glanced at my wedding ring. "Down that hall." She pointed. "Second room on the right."

I swam along the half-blue and beige corridor. Polyester clad staff swished by. John's father's long legs blocked the doorway of a small room. Slumped in an orange plastic chair, Van dozed. Balding with black glasses, he wore his navy blue nylon farm jacket with Michigan Blueberry Growers stamped above his heart. John's IV machine ticked beneath dim lights.

His room was an egg, thin white walls, white blanket, white bandages encased John's right hand. Breaking though the whiteness, I ran my ruddy hand across John's forehead, smoothing back his sandy-colored hair. His blue eyes focused on mine. His expression mirrored my anxiety of how this moment would sculpt our future.

"I'll never play music again," he said.

"Don't say that." My stomach tightened into a nutshell. My hands gripped the bed railing to quell their shaking. "We will fight."

Van stirred. "Oh, good, you're here. Think I'll go look for

a cup of coffee." He unfurled from the chair. His crepe soles squeaked across the linoleum.

"I'm sorry about all this." John reached for my hand. "Gosh, you're cold."

"Can't get warm. How'd it happen? I shrank into my ribs; shoulder muscles contracting, and avoided looking at the pink tint oozing into his bandages.

"The Log Splitter." John sounded the words as if he named the crocodile that bit off Captain Hook's hand. "Took part of my little finger too. I hopped on the tractor and made it to the folks' house. Van drove me to emergency in Douglas, but all they could do was sew up my hand. They told Van to go back for the finger and come up here. But this'll cost more."

"Musicians need *all* their fingers. Farmers, too."

That afternoon, I had eyed the log splitter, the steel piston, the red iron wedge, and the limp black hydraulic snakes connected to the tractor. The hired hand had built it to be operated by two people, one person to load the log, the other to snap the switch. I shuddered and closed my eyes. The glint of the piston flashed behind my eyelids. A current of blood stained a log and work boots.

"Hey, John," Lisa's voice parted the image. "Looks like they're taking good care of you." She bent over and rubbed his shoulder.

A pale man in a lab coat blew through the doorway, a white squall line; he pushed away the conversation and reminded us why we stood here.

"We're going to move your husband to surgery," the doctor

said. "It was a clean cut. Finger looks good." He nodded at a blue dishpan sitting on a counter.

Ice cubes surrounded John's third finger, cleansed of grease, dirt and blood. A fragment of flesh, a shard cracked from a granite boulder. What jumble of elements could bond bone and blood?

The floor quaked. Thunder boxed me ears. I sank onto a chair.

"Are you all right?" Lisa asked. "You look faint. Put your head down."

Head between my knees, I inhaled. That jagged shard of John rent the assumption that our bodies would plow the present and reap a future. We knew that someday aging would alter us, but at twenty-seven years, the adder of time had bit.

"Take her home," the doctor said. "Leave us your number. We'll call when the finger's on."

Lisa lifted me from the mire. Her hands buttoned my jacket. Her words, soft as lamb's wool, rubbed a hint of warmth into me. An arm around my waist, she threaded our way out the door and to her car.

"I'm taking you home with me." Lisa leaned into the backseat and pulled out an ice scraper.

The windshield wipers fanned away snow while Lisa brushed the car. The heater screamed. I wished it were last week; that yesterday would eclipse today and tomorrow. The car door slammed, and Lisa linked her seatbelt.

"How far is it from your place to John's folks' house?" Lisa asked.

"About a mile."

"Good thing John's big and strong. And thought quickly."

What had it felt like to shift with his left hand while holding his bleeding hand aloft? He had steered the tractor, talked with a doctor, thought through a decision and told his father where to find his finger. The same tenacity that battled droughts and insects was determined to reclaim his dexterity. But why hadn't I been there when he needed me?

At Lisa's house, her husband, Mark, hugged me. Short, slight of frame with dark hair, his fingers carved wood and fashioned spoons and snowshoes.

"Cloey's asleep," Mark said. "She went down about a half an hour ago."

Lisa opened the door to her toddler's room and peeked in. Protected by the lathes of her crib, fair-haired Chloe slumbered. A quarter of a mile away, Lake Michigan thrashed. Snow melted into the troughs of the waves where bits of ice clashed. The surf spewed spray that froze and encrusted the shore. As caretakers for a large church camp, Mark and Lisa dwelt on the pulse of the lake.

"Here." Lisa handed me an afghan. Mark set down cups of chamomile tea. We hunkered on the sofa, steam drifting about our cheeks. We chatted about Chloe's antics and whether winter had arrived to stay.

My ears listened; my mind crouched in the corner of the operating room. The doctor's fingers holding tiny forceps spliced together nerves and capillaries, coaxed flesh and bone into place. Supposedly the surgery would trick John's body into believing that his finger had never fallen into the snow. But what if the bone refused to knit? The flesh rejected the surgeon's stitches? The phone spoke, and Mark answered it.

"The finger's back on." Mark hung up the phone. "The nurse said that the doctor fastened it with a pin and re-attached the nerve endings, and the blood's flowing through normally. She said to go to bed."

"You can sleep in our spare room." Lisa stood up. "I'll take you home in the morning."

Snow hissed against the window. Lake Michigan thundered. I huddled beneath the blankets as a hemlock tree's branches scraped the roof. The night evaporated.

The next morning, Lisa dropped me off at home, and her car flitted away. Our gray tabby cat scolded me for abandoning him. I kindled a fire in the stove and held my hands over the radiant heat. But winds of fear still siphoned warmth from my flesh. If the early snow and cold lingered, how would we prepare for winter? Rolls of clear plastic sat on the porch, waiting to be tacked over single-paned windows. Wood to split, water to pump, and no John to share the load. Nor would he soon be able to lift an ax or pull the pump. Kitty placed his paws against my knees. I cuddled him against my shoulder.

Yet in Laura Ingalls Wilder's novel, *On the Banks of Plum Creek*, Ma Ingalls and her daughters had endured the blizzard while Pa huddled in the lee of the stream, burrowed in a snowy den. For four days, Ma had gripped a clothesline that ran between soddy and shed, stumbling through drifts to fetch wood and care for the livestock. She had outwitted the storm. I clutched Ma's hand, and drove to Grand Rapids.

Three flights of hospital stairs, and I scurried through another beige tunnel. The smell of antiseptic cleaner stalked me. In a room with mud puddle-colored walls John slept, his bandaged hand, a polar bear's paw, propped against his chest. The room begged for color. Pulling from my backpack a half-pieced quilt block and some scraps, I scattered wedges of gold, scarlet, purple and sage along the side of his bed. I stitched; John snored.

Finally, John's eyes opened. He moaned. Six foot two inches, two hundred pounds, toppled by a finger, a few ounces of flesh. John's hand could have existed without the digit, but daily he would have wondered why his finger would not respond when he reached across the accordion keys. He lifted his head.

"I'm sorry." He shifted his body and patted the edge of the bed with his other hand.

"I'm sorry, too." I scooted near him and kissed his cheek. He smelled too clean.

"All the driving to GR. All the work left undone."

Snowflakes splattered the window. Below, cars and trucks swam together and apart, flotsam on the evening flood.

"We'll manage. I probably should drive home before it's completely dark. Start a fire. Try to warm up the house."

Once cold permeates a house without central heating, it clings between the warp and the woof. Floorboards become frosty slabs. Canning jars emit waves of cold. Sheets freeze into slivers of ice. Like a hibernating bear, the house would resist, as the wood stove coaxed the rooms back to summer's warmth. I stuffed my quilting back into my backpack.

"Good idea," John reached one arm around me. "Water holding out?"

"I haven't used much, so haven't needed to pump any. See you tomorrow."

The cars' tires whirred through the slush as it crested the driveway and slid around the curve before halting. My wet boots trudged towards the dark house. A tangle of footprints spun through the front yard. Vandals? I followed the trails to the woodshed. A few golden chips littered the churned snow, but the logs had vanished. Split wood filled the shed. I ran up the porch steps. Warmth gushed through the front door. The black needle on the water gauge peaked at forty pounds of pressure. I collapsed in the rocker near the stove and cried, holding my fingers near the fire and thanking God for my friends.

Now, while John ate pineapples on a Honduran island, I once again wrapped my scarf around my face. Only my boots had pocked the paths this week. Dumping an armload of wood in the wood box, I stomped back to the woodshed for another. Three days until John would return, and there was only enough wood for two more days of warmth. I hefted his maul, but my arms could not raise it far enough to create the force necessary to cleave a log. I drove the hatchet used to split kindling into a small log, but it refused to crack.

Sunlight bounced off the drifts. Our wind generator would have whipped up electricity during the storm, but today's blaze needed to reach our solar panels and charge the battery bank, or I would sit in darkness. Once again, I dug a path to the big barn in order to reach the solar panels. I stomped up the stairs to the narrow side wing leading out to the hill, heaved the wooden door open, and sank to my waist. A sudden gust twirled white wraiths across the rise and shook an avalanche of snow off a nearby pine tree. A rainbow of ice cascaded over me, and I fell backwards. If I didn't move, would the cold claim me? When John returned, would he spy my red mittens reaching upward through a drift? I hacked out a trench, and crawled up to the flat roof of the battery room where the solar panels stood mute. Curtains of wrinkled snow encased the navy blue Plexiglas. I brushed away a foot of snow and gazed across the farm. I sat in the throat of a lily, white petals fanning outward.

Filmy cumulus clouds, the color of pearls, floated off the Lake. Because only a light breeze blew, the heat of the Lake drew air from both shores and towards her center. Her waves spun their moisture into a twist of wooly yarn that ran down her length and parallel to shore. Now the gray mass moved inland where the band of snow would unravel and dissipate. And out in the heart of the Lake, the waves twisted another strand of snow. I leaned against my snow shovel. How many more inches would I find tomorrow morning?

The following day, the blade on a red pick-up heaved a wave of white as a neighbor plowed our driveway. The truck stopped, rammed into drifts as it carved a path up the driveway. Freedom. Searching the woodshed, I pulled a few short pieces from where I had stuffed them in the gaps between larger logs. My boots crunched on the woodchips littering the shed's dirt floor, all that remained of John's labors. During evening chores, our goat Betsy pawed the straw, arranging her nest.

The next morning, sunshine warmed the goat shed as Betsy lay on her side, panting. The other two does stood near the stall's gate, bleating encouragement. Betsy grunted and two hooves emerged.

"Keep pushing," I said, stroking her stomach. From far off, I heard John's truck rumbling up the driveway.

The sound of an ax split Betsy's moan. *Whack*! Again, John's maul hit a log. Betsy heaved, and her kid tumbled into the sunlight.

A BAG OF BEES

A swarm in May is worth a load of hay
A swarm in June is worth a silver spoon.

One May afternoon while weeding my broccoli, I heard a loud buzzing moving towards me. I knew Carlos was checking his hives, so my first response was to flee from what I assumed were grouchy bees looking for a victim. But I've lived with a beekeeper long enough to know that May is a month when bees swarm, and beekeepers can increase their number of hives if they can catch a swarm. So before dashing for cover, I looked up and stared at the spiraling mass of honeybees flying over my head. I followed the humming cloud that rose over the trees surrounding our house, and paused outside of Carlos's bedroom window.

I groaned. Naturally these bees would come seeking my son who decorated his room with bee puppets and stuffed bee toys. I trotted off to find Carlos, knowing that we had only minutes before this swarm might take flight again. John noted my haste and hurried from the barn.

"Where's Carlos?" I asked. "There's a swarm knocking on his window."

John rolled his eyes. "Only for Carlos would a swarm come to him," he muttered.

At that moment we heard the rattle of our truck driven by our son in his white beekeeper suit. We blurted out the situation to Carlos, who followed us to the house.

The bees were spiraling into the characteristic cone they form as they protect the queen and choose a new home. Unfortunately their choice was the side of our chimney and the overhanging roof of our cantilevered house. We watched a few bees investigating cracks, intrepid spies sleuthing for a way into the house.

"Do something!" John said.

"Don't even think of keeping bees in your room," I said.

Calmly, Carlos fetched a ladder and placed a hive body on the roof of our porch, a short ways from the swarm. He inserted a few frames of comb that held a little honey.

"There, that should draw them down," Carlos said, and descended the ladder.

I ran upstairs where I could hear the beasties setting up housekeeping in our roof. A few of his nectar loving friends were flying inside Carlos' room, obvious the cleverest had spied the large wooden bee hanging from the ceiling.

After dinner we checked the swarm. It was smaller, but not because the bees had moved into the hive. Instead they were crawling farther into our roof. John and I shook our heads.

"What's next?" we asked.

"Well, I could wet them and stuff them into a paper sack." Carlos said.

"Yeah, right," I said.

"No, I read about this in *Bee Journal*. Some old beekeeper told about doing this. I'll need your spray bottle, a paper bag, and for you to open and close doors."

Carlos donned his bee veil and leather gloves, and climbed through a skylight and onto the roof. I watched from the skylight. He misted the crawling, buzzing mass. Heavy with water, the bees began to fall. He scooped handfuls into an open bag while speaking softly to his little buddies. The scene resembled a kind fireman rescuing a kitten from a tall tree rather than a beekeeper salvaging a swarm.

Finally the last of the cone filled the bag, and Carlos clasped together the ends of the sack. The safest descending route was through the large skylight and down the stairs. I opened and closed doors as he clutched the buzzing bag.

"They're a little angry," he said in his understated way.

"Did you get stung?" I asked the silly question that makes beekeepers wonder about the rest of us.

"A few times," Carlos said. Once outside, he hustled off to deposit the swarm in an empty hive.

I inspected his room where a few bees huddled in a little ball, high up by the ceiling. No doubt, Carlos would never notice them when he finally collapsed on his bed. After his exhibit of bravery, even I could tolerate a few insects in our home. But *only* for tonight.

BENCHMARK

I measure time by the day Matthew ran away. Unfolding a quilt, I try to remember if I created it before or after that moment in August? The red and cream pieces glow; the quilted feathers swirl across open spaces. No black interrupts its warmth. I sewed this one after we healed.

At the edge of a month roiling with Matthew's anger, our eighteen-year-old son looked up from eating lunch. Flint eyes, stiff jawed, defiance gushed from him.

"I'm leaving at five," he said.

My stomach clenched. My hands shook. Mercy, I prayed. Give us strength to wade through this storm.

The weariness of battling Matthew dimmed John's blue eyes. "Would you like to tell us where you are going?"

"No. It's none of your business."

I'll know where my dog sleeps tonight, but not my son? Ice chilled my veins. My body quivered. I set down my fork.

Carlos stared at his plate. Fear pooled in his face. At sixteen, he retained a sweet gentleness midst his emerging manhood.

"Ok," John said. "Do you want a suitcase?"

"No, just a garbage bag."

A black garbage bag, the perfect metaphor for how Matthew viewed himself. A rejected and abandoned child unable to claim the grace we extended through adoption.

"What about the bee business, your half of it?" John asked.

"Carlos can have it. All of it." Matthew shoved in his chair, strode to the screened in front porch, and laced up his work boots.

"You don't have to work this afternoon if you don't want to," John said.

He glanced at me, but I had nothing to give. The years of wrestling with Matthew's bitterness had left my heart as brittle as a milkweed pod.

Matthew grunted, slammed the screen door, and walked to John's pick-up.

I touched Carlos' shoulder. He shrugged me away, tied up his boots, and followed his brother.

"What should we do?" I asked.

"He's eighteen, we can't legally stop him. We need to shake berries. They're ripening fast and beginning to drop."

The August harvest did not acknowledge our heartache.

"Call a few friends and ask for prayers." John hugged me and headed out.

The growling of motors and the rattling of the shaker's rods drifted from the blueberry bog while I called friends. How many times over the past years had I begged them to pray for Matthew?

"Focus on Carlos," one friend said. "You're losing a son, but he's losing his only brother."

Out in my garden, my bare feet sank into the sandy soil. The scent of ripe tomatoes foreshadowed canning salsa and catsup. Zinnias blazed gold, red, and orange. Leaves brushed my face while I picked corn, and reduced the amount by four ears. Had Eden felt this way after the serpent lifted his head?

At four forty-five, John and Matthew walked into the house.

"Where's Carlos?" I surveyed John's haggard face.

"In the big barn." John hung up his battered straw hat and sank into a kitchen chair.

Matthew snatched a garbage bag and stalked to his room. He yanked out his dresser drawers and tossed in clothing. Standing just outside the boys' bedroom, I bit my lip when he added his Bible. Head up, he shoved us aside when we reached out to hug him, and stomped away.

John and I stood on the front porch watching our son march down the driveway. With his bag slung over a shoulder, Matthew walked around a curve and disappeared as he descended a hill. John leaned his head against the door jam and wept.

"I have to find Carlos." I ran to the barn.

Sobbing, Carlos sat on the steps to the second floor, his face pressed against the wooden railing. "He threatened over and over to run away, but I never thought he'd do it."

I wrapped my arms around him. "I'm so sorry. If there is anything I've done as a parent that hurt you, please forgive me. We tried to do our best."

"I know. It's alright. You did a good job."

His words stitched my wounds.

"Let's go to Dad," I said. With one arm around Carlos' shoulder, we plodded to the house and joined John on the sofa.

With Carlos between us, we gripped his hands and keened. Tears rolled down my neck and soaked my dress. Our corgi trotted to our feet and gazed up at us, absorbing our grief.

"While we were shaking berries this afternoon, a pair of Sandhill cranes flew over," John said. "Matthew called, 'Dad, Dad, look!' They flew so low we could hear their wings. This place will always be a part of him."

Carlos gulped and squashed a sob. "I need to tell you guys a few things."

He cast out a few petty misdeeds that he and Matthew had shared. I felt like a wretched parent for not noting my sons' evolving interests and needs.

"Don't worry about it," John said. "Typical boy stuff."

"And remember how he liked to wrestle?"

"What boys don't?" I said.

"But Matt would punch harder and harder. To get his way."

John and I locked eyes. Matthew had continually sought to control the family. Silently we vowed to do anything to help Carlos heal.

"What would you like to do this evening?" John asked. "Go to the lake?"

"We need to shake." Carlos rested his head on John's shoulder; the child who once could only relax on his father's chest migrated back for comfort.

"Are you sure you want to work?" I asked.

"Yes."

The farmer's panacea. Split wood. Hoe weeds. Stack lugs of fruit. Labor until the rhythm takes over, and mitigates the turmoil.

After supper, father and son harvested blueberries, yoked by grief and purpose. I sewed quilt blocks until the light faded.

Taking Flight

Like many small children, Carlos longed for wings. His yearnings were not prompted by super-heroes, but emanated from reading fairy tales, Peter Pan, and bird watching. He wanted to soar on gossamer wings and inhabit those worlds bright with bird song and youthful adventures.

John and I debated the merits of creating a pair of wings to enhance Carlos' playtime when he dwelt in his fantasy worlds. There was his Sand Colony dug into the side of a hill where his imaginary creatures lived, and the manor house for a toad that reminded Carlos of the rascal from *Wind in the Willows*. If we gave Carlos wings, could we trust our imaginative young son to differentiate between the real and pretend?

At last, we gave in. One afternoon I spread out a large remnant of black fabric, and Carlos lay on top of it so I could "measure" his wings. We had decided upon butterfly shaped wings that would be attached to straps like a on a backpack, and with elastic that he could slip onto his wrists.

My butterfly wanted to sparkle. Using household glue like

finger-paints; Carlos slathered the goop over the cloth so that it stiffened the fabric. Carlos also shook vials of glitter across his sticky wings. Swirls of gold, blue, red and green shimmered like Northern Lights. Later, we repeated the process on the other side of the wings, and for years afterwards I swept up glitter from between the cracks of the porch floorboards. While waiting for the glitter to dry, Carlos and I discussed how these were not *real* wings. He promised me that he would not attempt any flights from the peak of the barn; that he would only fly into those lands glowing in his mind.

And fly he did, from the picnic table, stumps, and other low take off stations. Carlos fluttered about the yard, and his mind sailed away as he twinkled and glittered in the sunshine. He wore his wings in the plays performed in our barn, and even shared them with playmates, all the while remembering that his wings were only for pretend.

Eventually Carlos hung the wings in his playhouse and threw himself into beekeeping. His eyes followed the wings of his bees and their honey, the liquid gold shining in glass jars. The summer after his freshman year in college, he often borrowed John's truck to haul trailers of hives. And he commented on every truck parked by the road with a for sale sign. John and I discussed the merits of investing in a used truck for Carlos and his growing business. Was he ready for this responsibility? We would appreciate not having to transport him back and forth from college. We reminded each other that Carlos had been careful with his first pair of wings.

The Sunday before Labor Day, Carlos' red truck gleamed in our driveway, packed with his youthful possessions, and a crateful of honey to sell on campus. His second year of college shimmered before him. After hugs and the usual request "to call us when you get there," he hopped into his truck and pulled away. About twenty yards from where John and I stood, we saw the flicker of his brake lights as Carlos paused and breathed in the richness of home one last time, before taking flight with his new wings.

TEAMWORK

"Then your light will rise in the darkness,
And your gloom will become like midday....
You will be like a well watered garden,
Like a spring of water whose waters do not fail."
Isaiah 58: 10-11

Standing in our sugar bush, tulip poplars and oaks towered above me. A south wind alluded to a shifting tempo as I snapped a maple twig. A single bead of sap clung to the exposed wood, sparkling in the sunlight then an inner current pulsed, and sap dribbled down the trunk. Like the red winged blackbird I heard yesterday, the flow of sap shoved aside the shadows of winter. I hustled to our orchard where John pruned apple trees.

"Saps running," I called. "We need to tap."

"Too early," John said. "Better wait a week." He lopped off a couple of suckers. We both knew bantering was part of our sugaring ritual, yet this year we faced shouldering the work without the help of our sons. While we didn't feel older, the question of who would eventually take over this farm rumbled in the back of our minds.

"But we'll miss this first run!"

John circled the tree, inspecting his work, maddeningly calm. Like that single bead of sap, I waited for that inner current to push John into sugaring season. He paused, and stared at the canopy of the woods, searching for the faintest red of swollen maple buds.

Finally, he slung his pruners under his arm. "All right. Let's load up."

We headed for the barn, where the goats with great swollen bellies rested in their stalls. Leo and Tolstoy lounged in the sun, their reddish brown fur shaggy from the winter cold. Steam rose off their backs and mixed with the odors of cattle, dung, and straw. The oxen struggled to erect themselves when John entered the paddock; their eyes followed their beloved teamster. Tolstoy nudged John, hoping for an apple; Leo extended his neck, seeking John's hand. An invisible power surged between John and his team.

"Time to go to work." John buckled halters about their massive heads, and led each ox to the hitching post. I entered the corral pocked by hoof prints filled, the mud sucking on my rubber boots. Reaching up, I curried Leo, the off ox who was slightly smaller than his teammate.

"Can you smell spring?" I murmured into his ear.

He shut his eyes and basked in the massage of the currycomb. His giant jaw sagged and drool spun from his chin. John lifted the wooden yoke across the shorthorns' shoulders. We each slipped a curved bow beneath their necks, and John inserted the pins that held the bows to the homemade yoke.

"Back," John commanded, and the team inched away from the hitching post. "Come," John called, and they moved toward the loaded bobsled while I latched the gate.

Like an expectant woman who has packed her bag and waits for the first contraction, a wooden bulk apple box filled with sap buckets sat on the sled. Wooden crates full of lids for the sap buckets flanked the bulk box, and two five-gallon plastic buckets containing spiles, a couple of hammers, and a brace-and-bit were wedged between the crates. John had patterned the bobsled after a rotting antique one abandoned by Dwight and Agnes Wadsworth. The salvaged ironware from the original sled now protected new burgundy stained runner boards. Leo and Tolstoy stepped back, and we attached the tongue of the sled to a ring in their yoke. As my hands held the wooden tongue, I wondered if perhaps Agnes had helped her husband hitch a team of Percherons to the original sled. Had the woman who left me apple orchards felt the same power of transformation when south winds thawed the soil?

"Come along!" John called. We marched out, and the wooden runners swooshed across the snow. John strode beside Tolstoy, the nigh ox, and encouraged his boys. A unique relationship develops between oxen and their driver as he trains them and works side by side. The teamster becomes the third member of the team.

"Good work! Good boys!" He shouted as we crested a small rise. "Haw now!" His felt-lined boots left larger footprints than the oxen's hooves. Years of splitting wood and loading hay had sculpted John's broad shoulders that swayed to the oxen's rhythm. Their leg muscles rippled as the oxen plodded through a drift that swamped my knees. Tolstoy's thick neck leaned against the yoke, while Leo strained to keep up. Castrated at three months, Leo had not developed a neck as thick or shoulders as broad as Tolstoy who was cut at one year. Their hoof steps thudded, and the earth quaked beneath their weight.

"Whoa!" John called. Leo and Tolstoy stopped beneath a cluster of maples and began to chew their cud.

John leaned against his brace and bit, and the drill dug into the sugar maple. Spirals of wood littered the snow as he sank the bit in about two inches. Sap oozed into the hole, and spilled down the bark in a thin stream. I followed behind John, carrying a bucket of spiles, and a hammer. I tapped each slim metal tube in about an inch and a half, and guided the hole in the rim of the sap bucket onto the spile. Finally, I slid on a dome-lid that would keep rain and snow out of the bucket.

"Plink, plank plunk," the sap drummed as it hit metal.

The staccato of a hairy woodpecker echoed throughout the woods and matched my hammering. Perched on the crest of a hill, John and I gazed across the ruddy rows of blueberry bushes that now stretched over forty acres. Neither of us spoke of the concerns pestering us, of whether the drought would continue during the growing season, or if frosts would once again claim most of our crops. We pushed those thoughts away, and reveled in the gift of the season and the sweetness of sharing labors.

"Should we tap this one?" John ran his hand along a young tree that was a sapling when we began sugaring twenty-five years ago. "Think it's big enough now?"

"Yes," I answered. An image of Carlos in his puffy beige snowsuit hovered in my mind. A small sand pail in his mitten-clad hand, he grasped the sapling while toddling toward me. Only a few years ago, the voices of our sons had flitted through the trees as they threw snowballs at their friends. Laughter had risen like the sap as young legs dashed from tree to tree, seeing who could carry the most buckets.

After John and I finished tapping one cluster of maples, he drove the oxen to the next gathering of trees. Leo nosed the ground, pulling up leaves, and the fragrance of wet earth. Tolstoy reached towards a tree, bringing up Leo's head, and they chomped at a branch overhanging the path. Traditionally, a drover is not supposed to allow his team to graze while they are yoked, but John broke off a pine branch and offered his boys a treat.

"I'll bring apples tonight," he said, scratching Tolstoy's head.

At the end of the afternoon, I hammered in the only remaining spile, and we hung the last of three hundred buckets. People often ask how many trees we tap, but because a large tree can sustain six taps, the real question is how many taps did you drill? Cold sharpened the clear, thin air as the setting sun turned the horizon apricot. I climbed into the empty bulk box, leaned against the rough wood, and anticipated setting my numb feet next to my cook stove.

The sled lurched forward and the runners rumbled over patches of freezing mud. My legs could propel me home faster, but the tramping of hooves and the creak of the yoke hinted at an earlier time in history. Most likely oxen hauled the wagon of the first family who settled this farm in 1837. Perhaps, Maria McCormick had wedged her spinning wheel and loom into the wagon, along with slips of old roses, and young apple trees wrapped in muslin.

Settlers used oxen for the same reasons we chose them. Calves are cheaper than horses, and a farmer can carve a yoke out of a log. Oxen are smart, and probably invented the idea that they were dumb in order to get out of working. Most oxen are easy to train; the first time Leo and Tolstoy were hooked to a wagon, they began to run. But after traveling hundred feet they realized that they were safe and walked on.

Smelling home, Leo and Tolstoy began to trot and John jogged next to them. The sled bounced, and I gripped the edges of the box. Chunks of snow flew from beneath the runners and muddy water sprayed from puddles.

"Whoa!" John called.

The team stopped. The sled jerked. Scooping me beneath the arms, John lifted me from my nest, set my feet on the ground, and kissed the back of my neck.

Hoar frost sparkled along the tree limbs the next morning. The moisture that the air had absorbed during yesterday's thaw had crystallized when the temperature fell into the twenties. By mid-afternoon, cumulus clouds flickered over us, blending sunshine and shadow, and long lines of honking geese flew north. The snowdrops and crocus by our house opened their petals. The sun pulled the sap up the maple trees, and the buckets overflowed. John loaded the collecting tank onto the bobsled.

"Would you like to stop by the cemetery first? I asked as we hitched Leo and Tolstoy to the sled. "See if they've brought your father's headstone?"

"No, too much work to do." John nudged Tolstoy. "Come!"

I gazed across the hay field towards the local cemetery, knowing that the frost of John's grief had not thawed. He still carried the ache alone. I wanted to remind him what I had said the day of his dad's death. *You did all you could for your father. You carried him to bed, tucked him in, and brought him a glass of water. You left him, thinking he would nap while on the other side of the wall you wrote checks and paid your parent's bills. You smiled at your mother, babbling words jumbled by Alzheimer's.* But instead, I walked behind him, watching the oxen swish their tails as we aimed for the woods.

Yesterday's sun had melted the path we broke, except where the runners had compressed the snow. There, like noodles, the tracks floated on the churned up fields. I searched the sky, and listened for the distant chortle of bluebirds, those vibrant friends that return in February. Each spring, their voices were part of a fugue that blended the tramp of the oxen, and the creaking of the wooden sled with the bluebirds' chortle.

Grasping five-gallon buckets, we stopped at every tree. I tipped each sap bucket, pouring the liquid into the gathering pail. Ice had formed overnight, and we skimmed it off, then stuffed our cold fingers back into our mittens. The Ottawa and Potawatomi, who once had camped on our farm, practiced this trick. Removing the ice increases the sugar content of the sap so that it will boil more quickly into syrup. Now and then, a sap bucket slipped from my grip and crashed into the five-gallon bucket, splashing my skirt and apron. The frigid wet seeped through the layers of petticoats, and I wondered how Maria McCormick had endured soaked hems.

Gatherings of snow fleas, tiny black insects, hopped about in the shallow prints of the oxen. Unlike tractor tires that cut ruts into the humus and leaf mold, the oxen's hooves leave only a hint of their passing. Beside me, a brown creeper moved up and down a maple, seeking the tiny white cocoons nestled between the ridges of bark. Sage green tinted the buds edging an elderberry branch, and violet leaves uncurled near the roots of an oak.

Other folks may run away from late winter, seeking the south's warmth, but I pity them. Nothing matches the mystery of sugaring. Although certain climatic conditions usually bring a good sap run, I've emptied full buckets while snow fell or fog drifted between the trees. Each run is a little bit like scanning the packages beneath a Christmas tree; will there be full buckets or only a couple of inches of sap?

Standing in a patch of sunshine, tails limp, Leo and Tolstoy dozed. Now and then an ear twitched. Our denim jackets absorbed the scent rising off their scruffy hides. John carried the full buckets back to the bobsled and poured the sap into the stock tank.

"Not a bad run," John said. "We'll measure the sugar content later." He stroked Tolstoy's jaw. "Back to work, boys."

With the stock tank filled, we plodded to the sugar shed, transferred the sap into a five-hundred gallon bulk tank, and returned to the woods to finish collecting. Snowmelt ran down the furrows in our driveway, coursing towards the pond in front of our house. Avalanches of snow crashed off the barn's tin roof, and settled into five-foot piles that would linger for weeks in the shade of the pines.

The next morning, a thin orange line separated earth and heaven. John's boots clumped up the porch steps as I flipped blueberry pancakes. He shoved open the front door.

"Tolstoy won't get up." His blue eyes were like a scared child's.

I slid the frying pan off the stove, snatched my jacket, and ran after John to the barn. Tolstoy's huge silhouette sprawled in the paddock. Leo sniffed his teammate, and nudged him with his head. Tolstoy remained rigid.

"We only hauled two loads yesterday. I didn't notice anything different about him. Did you?" John ran his hands over Tolstoy. "Stone cold."

"No, he seemed normal to me. What could've happened? He wasn't that old."

"I don't know. Heart attack, maybe." John's voice quavered.

Leo nuzzled John's back with his forehead as if asking, "What happened to my buddy? Why can't he get up?" Rose washed over the eastern sky, and bits of gold seeped through the clabbered clouds. Tolstoy's eyes stared without seeing the dawn.

"Do you want my help?" I asked after breakfast. "Should I call the vet?"

"I need to work alone." John pushed away his plate.

The vet confirmed our suspicions that Tolstoy probably died of a heart attack. From the porch, I watched John rumble into the pasture on his bulldozer. The front-end-loader ripped into the frozen earth. The machine growled as John shifted back and forth, scooping and dumping dirt. In the barn paddock, Leo circled

Tolstoy's body and lowed repeatedly. When the hole was deep enough for a one-ton ox, John approached Tolstoy and angled the dozer's bucket. Leo bellowed, and broke for the pasture. The caterpillar jerked, the hydraulic cylinders wheezed as they lifted the loaded bucket. Tolstoy's legs stuck out and the dark hooves chopped the sunlight streaming through the pines. John turned the dozer, and thundered toward the grave.

Leo zigzagged in front of the caterpillar, blocking its path; he plowed the ground with his head and tossed dust over his body. He bawled and raced toward the hole, pawing at the edge, attempting to jump. John hopped off and ran to Leo. He leaned his cheek against Leo's shoulder, and embraced him. With one hand John stroked Leo's chin while the other rubbed the ox's neck. Finally, John lifted his head and spoke. Leo shook his head. John drove Leo back to the paddock where he rested his arched neck on the fence and wailed, a deep fog horn. The caterpillar rolled.

A few minutes later, John stumbled into the house and shrugged off his jacket. His shoulders sagged as if he had shrunk. Tears glistened in his gray beard. I pulled him over to the sofa and held him. We cried, swaying ever so gently. He dug his forehead into the hollow of my neck.

"It's not *just* Tolstoy," he said, and trembled.

"I know." Tolstoy's horns had ripped through the hedge guarding John's heart. He wept for the sons who no longer work with him, shoulder to shoulder. For his father buried last summer. For the battles lost year after year to drought and disease when he watched his blueberry plants wither and die. For the silver lacing his hair, knowing that we were in the middle of our years, measuring the future and weighing the legacy that we would leave behind.

Epilogue: Leo never ceased pining for his teammate, and eventually he refused to eat, so our vet recommended that we put him to sleep. On a golden autumn afternoon, Leo rejoined Tolstoy. Now, they spend endless days munching grass and snoozing. Like after the loss of a beloved dog or cat, most of us say we will never have another pet, but one day, we miss the click of toenails upon the floor or a cat's tail weaving between our legs.

So a few years later, we welcomed a new team of shorthorn cattle to Pleasant Hill Farm. Once again, oxen race to the fence when John shows up with pumpkins for a fall treat. And sometimes, John strolls into the pasture where Buck and Henry lounge in the shade of the locust trees, sits down, and leans back against Buck. The three of them rest in the richness of their affection and memories of yesterday's work. And when the sap runs, we yoke up Buck and Henry, hitch them to the bobsled, and tramp into spring.

DISCUSSION QUESTIONS

1) Less than one percent of the United States' population now farms for a living, and only a fraction of that one percent are fruit farmers. What are the special challenges that fruit farmers face? What can we learn from their challenges?

2) Many farm workers are migrants; some could possibly be illegal immigrants. What do you think about employing migrants to harvest crops or should farmers seek local workers?

3) In the past dozen years, cow shares and community supported agriculture (CSA) have become household terms. Do you participate in any of these programs? Why or why not?

4) What did Wendell Berry mean when he alluded to agriculture as a "spiritual discipline"? What could we learn from the Benedictine monks, such as Thomas Merton, who are often involved in agriculture?

5) What are the parallels between the discipline of farming and other disciplines in our lives? Prayer and fasting? Practicing a musical instrument?

6) *The Christian Science Monitor* published an article in 2012 stating that over twenty-six percent of American households heat primarily with wood. Although methods of burning wood have improved, stoves still contribute over seventeen percent

of the fine particulates in air pollution. What can we do to continue utilizing wood, and still lower emissions?

7) In the past twenty-five years, the United States has suffered multiple droughts. What can each of us do to preserve water usage in agriculture or landscaping?

8) Not everyone can live off the electrical grid, but what are ways to capture solar and wind energy in the average home… such as clothes lines, solar radios and fans. What small ways do you harness solar or wind energy?

9) For over a decade, agricultural periodicals have reported the "graying" of American farmers. What can we do to encourage young people to embrace a lifestyle that often demands fourteen-hour days for months at a time?

Author's Note

Every year, countless visitors rumble up our driveway to tour our farm, pick blueberries, or purchase a bushel of peaches. As they open their car doors most exclaim about the farm's beauty, the splendor of the timber framed buildings, the fields of wild flowers, and the taste of our organic fruit.

"You are so lucky!" they say.

"No," I reply. "God has blessed us."

Organic farming is a challenging life. John and I have worked hard, but we realize that Pleasant Hill Farm is a gift of Grace. Throughout our almost forty years of growing fruit organically, our Lord has always provided whatever we needed…rain, physical strength, bumper crops midst the failures, and above all, a supportive community of family, friends and customers who with their families, return year after year. My Moravian ancestors lived in an eighteenth community called, *Gnadenhutten* which means "a place of grace," and that phrase describes our farm and our lives. My prayer is that these essays reflect that abundance and will heap blessings on you.

"For out of His abundance we have all received one grace after another and spiritual blessing upon spiritual blessing and even favor upon favor, and gift heaped upon gift."

John 1: 16 The Amplified Bible

For more information about our farm or my writing, please visit:

www.pleasanthillblueberryfarm.com or
www.joandonaldson.com.

At those sites, you can also view short videos that share tidbits from our barn parties and moments from the blueberry bog.

Or visit our Pleasant Hill Farm Facebook page where I write frequent updates about our agrarian activities. You can also listen to my recorded features about our farm on WMUK.org or read my Simple Living blog on Wordpress.com

CPSIA information can be obtained at www.ICGtesting.com
Printed in the USA
LVOW08s1406280314

379380LV00001B/50/P